Herons

Simon Stephens' first play, *Bring Me Sunshine*, was staged at the Assembly Rooms at the 1997 Edinburgh Fringe Festival, transferring to the Riverside Studios in London the same year. It was revived by the Royal Exchange in Manchester in 2000. His next play, *Bluebird*, was produced by the Royal Court in London in 1998 as part of their 'Choice' festival of new writing and received much critical acclaim. In 2000 he was the Arts Council Resident Dramatist at the Royal Court and the Pearson Attached Playwright at the Royal Exchange in Manchester.

Methuen

Published by Methuen 2001

1 3 5 7 9 10 8 6 4 2

First published in Great Britain in 2001 by
Methuen Publishing Limited
215 Vauxhall Bridge Road, London SW1V 1EJ

Methuen Publishing Limited Reg. No. 3543167

A CIP catalogue record for this book is available from the British Library.

ISBN 0 413 76370 6

Typeset by SX Composing DTP, Rayleigh, Essex
Printed and bound in Great Britain by
Cox & Wyman Ltd, Reading, Berkshire

ROYAL COURT

Royal Court Theatre presents

HERONS

by Simon Stephens

First performance at the Royal Court Jerwood Theatre Upstairs,
Sloane Square, London on 18 May 2001.

Supported by Jerwood New Playwrights.

HERONS

by **Simon Stephens**

Cast in order of appearance
Billy Lee Russell **Billy Seymour**
Scott Cooper **Robert Boulter**
Aaron Riley **Stuart Morris**
Darren Madden **Ryan Winsley**
Adele Kent **Lia Saville**
Charlie Russell **Nicolas Tennant**
Michelle Russell **Jane Hazlegrove**

Director **Simon Usher**
Designer **Antony Lamble**
Lighting Designer **Paul Russell**
Sound Designer **Ian Dickinson**
Casting **Lisa Makin, Amy Ball**
Production Manager **Sue Bird**
Company Stage Manager **Cath Binks**
Stage Management **Suzanne Bourke, Louise McDermott**
Stage Management Work Placement **Dani Youngman**
Costume Supervisor **Suzanne Duffy**
Voice Coach **Patsy Rodenburg**

Royal Court Theatre would like to thank the following for their help with this production:
Fishing Equipment from Sharpe's of Aberdeen, London, Imperial Tobacco Limited Hogshead, Islington,
Wardrobe care by Persil and Comfort courtesy of Lever Brothers Ltd.

JERWOOD
NEW PLAYWRIGHTS

Since 1993 Jerwood New Playwrights have contributed to some of the Royal Court's most successful productions, including SHOPPING AND FUCKING by Mark Ravenhill (co-production with Out of Joint), EAST IS EAST by Ayub Khan-Din (co-production with Tamasha), THE BEAUTY QUEEN OF LEENANE by Martin McDonagh (co-production with Druid Theatre Company), THE WEIR by Conor McPherson, REAL CLASSY AFFAIR by Nick Grosso, THE FORCE OF CHANGE by Gary Mitchell, ON RAFTERY'S HILL by Marina Carr (co-production with Druid Theatre Company),4.48 PSYCHOSIS by Sarah Kane and UNDER THE BLUE SKY by David Eldridge.

The Jerwood Charitable Foundation is a registered charity dedicated to imaginative and responsible funding and sponsorship of the arts, education, design and other areas of human endeavour and excellence. This season Jerwood New Playwrights are supporting PRESENCE by David Harrower, HERONS by Simon Stephens and CLUBLAND by Roy Williams.

www.jerwood.org.uk

UNDER THE BLUE SKY by David Eldridge
(photo: Ivan Kyncl)

EAST IS EAST by Ayub Khan-Din
(photo: Robert Day)

THE COMPANY

Simon Stephens (writer)
For the Royal Court: Bluebird (Choice Festival, 1998).
Other theatre includes: Bring Me Sunshine (Assembly Rooms, 1997 Edinburgh Fringe Festival and revived Manchester Royal Exchange, 2000). Simon's radio play William Curran is due to be broadcast by Radio 4 in September.
He also received a Pearson Bursary at the Manchester Royal Exchange and was the Arts Council Resident Dramatist at the Royal Court in 2000.

Robert Boulter
Theatre includes: Runaways (Questors); Grease, Little Shop of Horrors (Watford).
Television includes: The Bill, TV commercials.

Ian Dickinson (sound designer)
Theatre includes: Search and Destroy (New End, Hampstead); Phaedra, Three Sisters, The Shaughraun, Writer's Cramp (Royal Lyceum, Edinburgh); The Whore's Dream (RSC Fringe, Edinburgh); As You Like It, An Experienced Woman Gives Advice, Present Laughter, The Philadelphia Story, Wolks World, Poor Superman, Martin Yesterday, Fast Food, Coyote Ugly, Prizenight (Royal Exchange, Manchester); Great Monsters of Western Street (Throat Theatre Company); Small Craft Warnings, Tieble and Her Demon (Manchester Evening News Theatre Awards Best Design Team), The Merchant of Venice, Death and The Maiden (Library Theatre Company, Manchester).
Ian is Sound Deputy at the Royal Court.

Jane Hazlegrove
Theatre includes: Snake in the Grass (Old Vic); Wishbones, Boom Bang-a-Bang, The Mortal Ash (Bush); The Wolves (Paines Plough tour); Heartbreak House (Coventry); My Mother Said I Never Should, Blood Wedding (Bolton); The Crucible (Manchester Library); To Kill a Mockingbird (Manchester Contact).
Television includes: Without Motive, The Cops, Hero to Zero, Big Smoke, Jonathan Creek, Shooting Star.
Film includes: Heidi, The Whipping Boy, The River Esk Triumph.

Anthony Lamble (designer)
Theatre includes: The Contractor, Troilus and Cressida (Oxford Stage Company); The Sea, Aristocrats, The Retreat from Moscow, The School of Night, Insignificance, The King of Prussia (Minerva, Chichester); A Midsummer Night's Dream, As You Like It (RNT and tour); Lettice and Lovage, Burning Everest, Exquisite Sister (West Yorkshire Playhouse); Card Boys, All of You Mine, Mortal Ash, Pondlife (Bush). Anthony has also designed productions for Leicester Haymarket, Sheffield Crucible, Almeida Music Festival, English Touring Theatre, Belgrade, Coventry, The Gate, Riverside Studios, Lyric Hammersmith, Shared Experience, Paines Plough and RSC Pit.
Opera includes: Palace in the Sky (Hackney Empire for the ENO/Lilian Baylis Programme), L'Orfeo (Purcell Quartet, Japanese tour).
Film includes: A Secret Audience.
Anthony is a course tutor for the Motley Theatre Design Course.

Stuart Morris
Theatre includes: Oliver (London Palladium); Dick Daredevil (Drill Hall).
Television includes: Home Farm Twins, Monsignor Renard, Casualty, London's Burning, Anything's Possible, Shane Ritchie Experience, Middlemarch, The Tony Ferrino Phenomenon, Eastenders, Disney Club, Crimewatch, Get Your Act Together.
Radio includes: Fun Filled Days of Harriet Night, First Steps in Drama.

Paul Russell (lighting designer)
For the Royal Court: Not a Game for Boys.
Other theatre includes: Hard Times (Watermill,
Newbury); Closer (RNT international tour);
Madame Butterfly (Singapore Repertory
Theatre); Trainspotting, Raising Fires, One Flea
Spare (amongst many other productions at the
Bush); The Way You Look Tonight (Druid);
Exodus (Tara Arts); The Cherry Orchard
(Guildhall); Danton's Death, The Portuguese
Boat Plays, The Great Highway, Rousseau's Tale,
Bad Blood, Picnic /Guernica, Talking Tongues,
Anowa, Dear Elena Sergeievna, Silver Face,
Hunting Scenes in Lower Bavaria (Gate);
Madness in Valencia, The Great Pretenders (Gate
and tour); Fat Janet, Iona Rain (Croydon
Warehouse); Peribanez (Cambridge Arts); The
Wolves (Paines Plough tour); My Mother Said I
Never Should (Oxford Stage Co); Yiddish Trojan
Woman (Cockpit); Boy (Everyman
Liverpool/Lyric Hammersmith/BAC and national
tour); Love at a Loss (BAC and national tour); Mr
Director (Orange Tree); Theaker Dance (Palace
and tour); Webster (Old Red Lion); The Eleventh
Commandment (Hampstead); Max Clapper
(Electric Cinema); Exquisite Sister (West
Yorkshire Playhouse/Edinburgh festival); Musical
Scenes (BAC); Pig's Ear (Liverpool Playhouse)
Opera includes: Snatched by the Gods, Broken
Strings (Almeida), Linda Di Chamonix, Rape of
Lucretia (Guildhall), Cosi Fan Tutti (Ealing), West
Side Story (Pimlico Opera at Wandsworth
Prison).
Paul is Resident Production Manager at the
Young Vic.

Lia Saville
Theatre includes: Annie (Victoria Palace); Oliver
(London Palladium); Whistle Down the Wind
(Sydmenton Festival).
Television includes: Pig Heart Boy, See Saw, Black
Britain, Eastenders, Live and Kicking.

Billy Seymour
Herons is Billy's first professional theatre
production.
Television includes: A Christmas Carol,
Brainfood, Modern Times, The Pig Boy,
TV commercials.

Nicolas Tennant
Theatre includes: Les Justes (Gate); The
Recruiting Officer (Chichester Festival); King
Lear (RSC); Little Malcolm and His Struggle
Against The Eunuchs (Hampstead); Sugar, Sugar,
Love and Understanding (Bush); New Play
Festival (Derby); Henry IV, I & II (ETT tour and
Old Vic); Not a Game for Boys (RNT tour and
Edinburgh Festival 98); The Blue Ball, Billy Liar
(RNT); Bad Company (RNT Studio and Bush);
Sailor Beware (Queen's, Hornchurch and tour);
Soundings (Old Red Lion); Inventing a New
Colour (Northcott Theatre, Exeter); Billy Budd
(Crucible, Sheffield); K-Top, The Trouble with
Girls (RNT Studio).
Television includes: Residents, The Bill,
Eastenders, Back-up, The Bombmaker,
Between the Lines, Friday on My Mind, Trainer,
Nice Town.
Film includes: Tube Tales, Oscar and Lucinda,
Backbeat, The Gift, The Fool, A Dangerous
Man.

Simon Usher (director)
Theatre includes: Looking at You (Revived)
Again, The Evil Doers, Pond Life, Not Fade
Away, The Mortal Ash, All of You Mine,
Wishbones, Card Boys (Bush); King Baby (RSC,
Pit); The War in Heaven, Timon of Athens,
Pericles, The Winter's Tale, The Broken Heart,
The Lover' s Melancholy, French Without Tears,
The Bells, Pale Performer, Trios, Lettice and
Lovage, The Naked, Murders in the Rue
Morgue (Haymarket, Leicester); Waiting for
Godot, The Browning Version, Heartbreak
House, Hamlet, Les Liaisons Dangereuses,
Whole Lotta Shakin' (Belgrade, Coventry); No
Man's Land (English Touring Theatre); Mr
Puntila and His Man Matti (Chichester); Can't
Stand Up for Falling Down (Watford Palace and
tour); Burning Everest, Exquisite Sister (West
Yorkshire Playhouse); The Wolves (Paines
Plough); Twins (Birmingham Rep); Great Balls of
Fire (Cambridge theatre, West End).

Ryan Winsley
Herons is Ryan's first professional production.

THE ENGLISH STAGE COMPANY AT THE ROYAL COURT

The English Stage Company at the Royal Court opened in 1956 as a subsidised theatre producing new British plays, international plays and some classical revivals.

The first artistic director George Devine aimed to create a writers' theatre, 'a place where the dramatist is acknowledged as the fundamental creative force in the theatre and where the play is more important than the actors, the director, the designer'. The urgent need was to find a contemporary style in which the play, the acting, direction and design are all combined. He believed that 'the battle will be a long one to continue to create the right conditions for writers to work in'.

Devine aimed to discover 'hard-hitting, uncompromising writers whose plays are stimulating, provocative and exciting'. The Royal Court production of John Osborne's Look Back in Anger in May 1956 is now seen as the decisive starting point of modern British drama and the policy created a new generation of British playwrights. The first wave included John Osborne, Arnold Wesker, John Arden, Ann Jellicoe, N F Simpson and Edward Bond. Early seasons included new international plays by Bertolt Brecht, Eugène Ionesco, Samuel Beckett, Jean-Paul Sartre and Marguerite Duras.

The theatre started with the 400-seat proscenium arch Theatre Downstairs, and then in 1969 opened a second theatre, the 60-seat studio Theatre Upstairs. Productions in the Theatre Upstairs have transferred to the West End, such as Caryl Churchill's Far Away, Conor McPherson's The Weir, Kevin Elyot's My Night With Reg and Ariel Dorfman's Death and the Maiden. The Royal Court also co-produces plays which have transferred to the West End or toured internationally, such as Sebastian Barry's The Steward of Christendom and Mark Ravenhill's Shopping and Fucking (with Out of Joint), Martin McDonagh's The Beauty Queen Of Leenane (with Druid Theatre Company), Ayub Khan-Din's East is East (with Tamasha Theatre Company, and now a feature film).

Since 1994 the Royal Court's artistic policy has again been vigorously directed to finding and producing a new generation of playwrights. The writers include Joe Penhall, Rebecca Prichard, Michael Wynne, Nick Grosso, Judy Upton, Meredith Oakes, Sarah Kane, Anthony Neilson, Judith Johnson, James Stock, Jez Butterworth, Marina Carr, Simon Block, Martin McDonagh, Mark Ravenhill, Ayub Khan-Din, Tamantha Hammerschlag, Jess Walters, Che Walker, Conor McPherson, Simon Stephens, Richard Bean, Roy

photo: Andy Chopping

Williams, Gary Mitchell, Mick Mahoney, Rebecca Gilman, Christopher Shinn, Kia Corthron, David Gieselmann, Marius von Mayenburg and David Eldridge. This expanded programme of new plays has been made possible through the support of A.S.K Theater Projects, the Jerwood Charitable Foundation, the American Friends of the Royal Court Theatre and many in association with the Royal National Theatre Studio.

In recent years there have been record-breaking productions at the box office, with capacity houses for Jez Butterworth's Mojo, Sebastian Barry's The Steward of Christendom, Martin McDonagh's The Beauty Queen of Leenane, Ayub Khan-Din's East is East, Eugène Ionesco's The Chairs, David Hare's My Zinc Bed and Conor McPherson's The Weir, which transferred to the West End in October 1998 and ran for nearly two years at the Duke of York's Theatre.

The newly refurbished theatre in Sloane Square opened in February 2000, with a policy still inspired by the first artistic director George Devine. The Royal Court is an international theatre for new plays and new playwrights, and the work shapes contemporary drama in Britain and overseas.

REBUILDING THE ROYAL COURT

In 1995, the Royal Court was awarded a National Lottery grant through the Arts Council of England, to pay for three quarters of a £26m project to completely rebuild our 100-year old home. The rules of the award required the Royal Court to raise £7.6m in partnership funding. The building has been completed thanks to the generous support of those listed below.

We are particularly grateful for the contributions of over 5,700 audience members.

Royal Court Registered Charity number 231242.

THE AMERICAN FRIENDS OF THE ROYAL COURT THEATRE

AFRCT support the mission of the Royal Court and are primarily focused on raising funds to enable the theatre to produce new work by emerging American writers. Since this not-for-profit organisation was founded in 1997, AFRCT has contributed to seven productions including Rebecca Gilman's Spinning Into Butter. They have also supported the participation of young artists in the Royal Court's acclaimed International Residency.

If you would like to support the ongoing work of the Royal Court, please contact the Development Department on 020 7565 5050.

ROYAL COURT
DEVELOPMENT BOARD
Tamara Ingram (Chair)
Jonathan Cameron (Vice Chair)
Timothy Burrill
Anthony Burton
Jonathan Caplan QC
Joyce Hytner
Mary Ellen Johnson
Dany Khosrovani
Dan Klein
Feona McEwan
Michael Potter
Sue Stapely

PRINCIPAL DONOR
Jerwood Foundation

WRITERS CIRCLE
The Cadogan Estate
Carillon/Schal
News International plc
Pathé
The Eva and Hans K Rausing Trust
The Rayne Foundation
Sky
Garfield Weston Foundation

DIRECTORS CIRCLE
The Esmée Fairbairn Charitable Trust
The Granada Group plc

ACTORS CIRCLE
Edwin C Cohen & The Blessing Way Foundation
Ronald Cohen & Sharon Harel-Cohen
Quercus Charitable Trust
The Basil Samuel Charitable Trust
The Trusthouse Charitable Foundation
The Woodward Charitable Trust

SPECIFIC DONATIONS
The Foundation for Sport and the Arts for Stage System
John Lewis Partnership plc for Balcony
City Parochial Foundation for Infra Red Induction Loops and Toilets for Disabled Patrons

RSA Art for Architecture Award Scheme for Antoni Malinowski Wall Painting

AMERICAN FRIENDS

Founders
Harry Brown
Victoria Elenowitz
Francis Finlay
Monica Gerard-Sharp
The Howard Gilman Foundation
Jeananne Hauswald
Mary Ellen Johnson
Dany Khosrovani
Kay Koplovitz
The Laura Pels Foundation
Stephen Magowan
Monica Menell-Kinberg Ph.D.
Benjamin Rauch
Rory Riggs
Robert Rosenkranz
Gerald Schoenfeld, The Shubert Organization

Patrons
Daniel Baudendistel
Arthur Bellinzoni
Miriam Bienstock
Robert L & Janice Billingsley
Catherine G Curran
Leni Darrow
Michael & Linda Donovan
Ursula & William Fairbairn
April Foley
Amanda Foreman
Mr & Mrs Richard Gelfond
Mr & Mrs Richard Grand
Mr & Mrs Paul Hallingby
Sharon King Hoge
The Carl C Icahn Family Foundation
Maurice & Jean R Jacobs
Mr & Mrs Ernest Kafka
Sahra T Lese
Susan & Martin Lipton
Eleanor Margolis
Hamish & Georgone Maxwell
Kathleen O'Grady
Howard & Barbara Sloan

Margaret Jackson Smith
Mika Sterling
Arielle Tepper
The Thorne Foundation

Benefactors
Mr & Mrs Tom Armstrong
Mr & Mrs Mark Arnold
Elaine Attias
Rachael Bail
Mr & Mrs Matthew Chapman
David Day
Richard & Rosalind Edelman
Abe & Florence Elenowitz
Hiram & Barbara Gordon
Mr & Mrs Brian Keelan
Jennifer C E Laing
Burt Lerner
Imelda Liddiard
Dr Anne Locksley
Mr & Mrs Rudolph Rauch
Lawrence & Helen Remmel
Mr & Mrs Robert Rosenberg
Mr & Mrs William Russell
Harold Sanditen
Mr & Mrs Robert Scully
Julie Talen
Mr & Mrs Charles Whitman

THE ARTS COUNCIL OF ENGLAND

PROGRAMME SUPPORTERS

The Royal Court (English Stage Company Ltd) receives its principal funding from London Arts. It is also supported financially by a wide range of private companies and public bodies and earns the remainder of its income from the box office and its own trading activities.
The Royal Borough of Kensington & Chelsea gives an annual grant to the Royal Court Young Writers' Programme and the London Boroughs Grants Committee provides project funding for a number of play development initiatives.

The Jerwood Charitable Foundation continues to support new plays by new playwrights through the Jerwood New Playwrights series. Since 1993 the A.S.K. Theater Projects of Los Angeles has funded a Playwrights' Programme at the theatre. Bloomberg Mondays, the Royal Court's reduced price ticket scheme, is supported by Bloomberg.
Sky has also generously committed to a two-year sponsorship of the Royal Court Young Writers' Festival.

TRUSTS AND FOUNDATIONS
American Friends of the Royal Court Theatre
The Carnegie United Kingdom Trust
Carlton Television Trust
Gerald Chapman Fund
Cultural Foundation Deutsche Bank
The Foundation for Sport and The Arts
The Genesis Foundation
The Goldsmiths Company
Jerwood Charitable Foundation
The John Lyons Charity
Laura Pels Foundation
Quercus Charitable Trust
The Peggy Ramsay Foundation
The Peter Sharp Foundation
The Royal Victoria Hall Foundation
The Sobell Foundation
The Trusthouse Charitable Foundation
Garfield Weston Foundation

MAJOR SPONSORS
A.S.K. Theater Projects
AT&T
Barclays plc
Bloomberg
Credit Suisse First Boston
Francis Finlay
Lever Fabergé (through Arts & Business New Partners)
Royal College of Psychiatrists
Sky

BUSINESS MEMBERS
Laporte plc
LAZARD
Lever Fabergé
McCABES
Pemberton Greenish
Peter Jones
Redwood Publishing
Simons Muirhead & Burton
J Walter Thompson

INDIVIDUAL MEMBERS
Patrons
Anon
David H Adams
Advanpress

Katie Bradford
Mrs Alan Campbell-Johnson
Gill Carrick
David Coppard
Chris Corbin
David Day
Greg Dyke
Thomas Fenton
Ralph A Fields
John Flower
Mike Frain
Edna & Peter Goldstein
David R & Catherine Graham
Phil Hobbs
Homevale Ltd
Mr & Mrs Jack Keenan
JHJ & SF Lewis
Lex Service plc
Barbara Minto
Michael & Mimi Naughton
New Penny Productions Ltd
Martin Newson
AT Poeton & Son Ltd.
André Ptaszynski, Really Useful Theatres
Carolin Quentin
David Rowland
Sir George Russell
Ian Sellars
Bernard Shapero
Miriam Stoppard
Carl & Martha Tack
Jan & Michael Topham
Mr & Mrs Anthony Weldon
Richard Wilson OBE

Benefactors
Anon
Anastasia Alexander
Lesley E Alexander
Judith Asalache
Batia Asher
Elaine Mitchell Attias
Thomas Bendhem
Mark Bentley
Jody Berger
Keith & Helen Bolderson
Jeremy Bond
Brian Boylan
Mr & Mrs F H Bradley III
Mrs Elly Brook JP
Julian Brookstone
Paul & Ossi Burger
Debbi & Richard Burston
Yuen-Wei Chew
Martin Cliff

Carole & Neville Conrad
Conway Van Gelder
Coppard & Co.
Barry Cox
Curtis Brown Ltd
Deborah Davis
Zöe Dominic
Robyn Durie
Lorraine Esdaile
Winston & Jean Fletcher
Claire & William Frankel
Nick Fraser
Robert Freeman
J Garcia
Beverley & Nathaniel Gee
Norman Gerard
Henny Gestetner OBE
Jacqueline & Jonathan Gestetner
Michael Goddard
Carolyn Goldbart
Judy & Frank Grace
Sally Greene
Byron Grote
Sue & Don Guiney
Hamilton Asper Management
Woodley Hapgood
Jan Harris
Anna Home OBE
Amanda Howard Associates
Trevor Ingman
Lisa Irwin-Burgess
Peter Jones
Paul Kaju & Jane Peterson
Peter & Maria Kellner
Diana King
Clico Kingsbury
Lee & Thompson
Caroline & Robert Lee
C A Leng
Lady Lever
Colette & Peter Levy
Ann Lewis
Ian Mankin
Christopher Marcus
David Marks
Nicola McFarland
James McIvor
Mr & Mrs Roderick R McManigal
Mae Modiano
Eva Monley
Pat Morton
Georgia Oetker
Paul Oppenheimer

Janet & Michael Orr
Maria Peacock
Pauline Pinder
JTG Philipson QC
Jeremy Priestley
John & Rosemarie Reynolds
John Ritchie
Samuel French Ltd
Bernice & Victor Sandelson
John Sandoe (Books) Ltd
Nicholas Selmes
Lois Sieff OBE
Peregrine Simon
David & Patricia Smalley
Brian D Smith
John Soderquist
Max Stafford-Clark
Sue Stapely
Ann Marie Starr
June Summerill
Anthony Wigram
George & Moira Yip

STAGE HANDS CIRCLE
Graham Billing
Andrew Cryer
Lindy Fletcher
Susan Hayden
Mr R Hopkins
Philip Hughes Trust
Dr A V Jones
Roger Jospe
Miss A Lind-Smith
Mr J Mills
Nevin Charitable Trust
Janet & Michael Orr
Jeremy Priestley
Ann Scurfield
Brian Smith
Harry Streets
Richard Wilson OBE
C C Wright

AWARDS FOR
THE ROYAL COURT

Terry Johnson's Hysteria won the 1994 Olivier Award for Best Comedy, and also the Writers' Guild Award for Best West End Play. Kevin Elyot's My Night with Reg won the 1994 Writers' Guild Award for Best Fringe Play, the Evening Standard Award for Best Comedy, and the 1994 Olivier Award for Best Comedy. Joe Penhall was joint winner of the 1994 John Whiting Award for Some Voices. Sebastian Barry won the 1995 Writers' Guild Award for Best Fringe Play, the 1995 Critics' Circle Award and the 1997 Christopher Ewart-Biggs Literary Prize for The Steward of Christendom, and the 1995 Lloyds Private Banking Playwright of the Year Award. Jez Butterworth won the 1995 George Devine Award for Most Promising Playwright, the 1995 Writers' Guild New Writer of the Year Award, the Evening Standard Award for Most Promising Playwright and the 1995 Olivier Award for Best Comedy for Mojo.

The Royal Court won the 1995 Prudential Award for Theatre and was the overall winner of the 1995 Prudential Award for the Arts for creativity, excellence, innovation and accessibility. The Royal Court Theatre Upstairs won the 1995 Peter Brook Empty Space Award for innovation and excellence in theatre.

Michael Wynne won the 1996 Meyer-Whitworth Award for The Knocky. Martin McDonagh won the 1996 George Devine Award, the 1996 Writers' Guild Best Fringe Play Award, the 1996 Critics' Circle Award and the 1996 Evening Standard Award for Most Promising Playwright for The Beauty Queen of Leenane. Marina Carr won the 19th Susan Smith Blackburn Prize (1996/7) for Portia Coughlan. Conor McPherson won the 1997 George Devine Award, the 1997 Critics' Circle Award and the 1997 Evening Standard Award for Most Promising Playwright for The Weir. Ayub Khan-Din won the 1997 Writers' Guild Award for Best West End Play, the 1997 Writers' Guild New Writer of the Year Award and the 1996 John Whiting Award for East is East. Anthony Neilson won the 1997 Writers' Guild Award for Best Fringe Play for The Censor.

At the 1998 Tony Awards, Martin McDonagh's The Beauty Queen of Leenane (co-production with Druid Theatre Company) won four awards including Garry Hynes for Best Director and was nominated for a further two. Eugene Ionesco's The Chairs (co-production with Theatre de Complicite) was nominated for six Tony awards. David Hare won the 1998 Time Out Live Award for Outstanding Achievement and six awards in New York including the Drama League, Drama Desk and New York Critics Circle Award for Via Dolorosa. Sarah Kane won the 1998 Arts Foundation Fellowship in Playwriting. Rebecca Prichard won the 1998 Critics' Circle Award for Most Promising Playwright for Yard Gal (co-production with Clean Break).

Conor McPherson won the 1999 Olivier Award for Best New Play for The Weir. The Royal Court won the 1999 ITI Award for Excellence in International Theatre. Sarah Kane's Cleansed was judged Best Foreign Language Play in 1999 by Theater Heute in Germany. Gary Mitchell won the 1999 Pearson Best Play Award for Trust. Rebecca Gilman was joint winner of the 1999 George Devine Award and won the 1999 Evening Standard Award for Most Promising Playwright for The Glory of Living.

Roy Williams and Gary Mitchell were joint winners of the George Devine Award 2000 for Most Promising Playwright for Lift Off and The Force of Change respectively. At the Barclays Theatre Awards 2000 presented by the TMA, Richard Wilson won the Best Director Award for David Gieselmann's Mr Kolpert and Jeremy Herbert won the Best Designer Award for Sarah Kane's 4.48 Psychosis. Gary Mitchell won the Evening Standard's Charles Wintour Award 2000 for Most Promising Playwright for The Force of Change. Stephen Jeffreys' I Just Stopped by to See The Man won an AT&T: On Stage Award 2000. David Eldridge's Under the Blue Sky won the Time Out Live Award 2001 for Best New Play in the West End.

In 1999, the Royal Court won the European theatre prize New Theatrical Realities, presented at Taormina Arte in Sicily, for its efforts in recent years in discovering and producing the work of young British dramatists.

ROYAL COURT BOOKSHOP

The bookshop offers a wide range of playtexts, theatre books, screenplays and art-house videos with over 1,000 titles. Located in the downstairs Bar and Food area, the bookshop is open Monday to Saturday, afternoons and evenings.

Many Royal Court playtexts are available for just £2 including the plays in the current season and recent works by David Hare, Conor McPherson, Martin Crimp, Sarah Kane, David Mamet, Gary Mitchell, Martin McDonagh, Ayub Khan-Din, Jim Cartwright and Rebecca Prichard. We offer a 10% reduction to students on a range of titles.
Further information : 020 7565 5024

FOR THE ROYAL COURT

Royal Court Theatre
Sloane Square, London SW1W 8AS
Tel: 020 7565 5050 Fax: 020 7565 5001
info@royalcourttheatre.com
www.royalcourttheatre.com

Herons

Characters

Billy Lee Russell   *Fourteen years old. A dirty, scruffed mop of hair. Wears a thin and old Adidas jacket and a Nike Air baseball cap. He speaks in the manner of somebody with a desperate eagerness to please, to satisfy, to explain, to charm others. This eagerness manifests itself also in the way that he moves.*

Charlie Russell   *Thirty-four years old. Billy's father. A hulking damaged man in his mid-thirties. He wears a blue jacket over a white T-shirt and jeans and he smokes rolled up cigarettes with remarkable constancy. His skill at rolling these cigarettes betrays surprising subtlety and dexterity. Charlie trips over his words when he talks, as though he can't possibly explain everything that he needs to. This struggle results in inarticulacy. And occasional accidental poetry. He is a man who has watched bewildered as almost everything that he once loved has been taken away from him.*

Michelle Russell   *Thirty-two years old. Billy's mother. Separated from Charlie. She has a confident energy that she struggles to contain when she speaks to Billy, almost out of fear of frightening him. She takes great care over her appearance but there is something about her clothes, particularly about the coat she wears, which is somehow awkward. It is as though she is trying too hard. She can look, at times, monumentally tired.*

Adele Kent   *Thirteen years old. She is a year below Billy in school. She wears her school uniform still. She wears it unruly. She has a disarming directness. She has bleached blonde hair and dark eyes. She has something of a reputation around and outside of the school – not for being feared, but she is respected. She is a friend of Scott Cooper's. Scott does not know she has taken to visiting Billy. At first she makes Billy nervous.*

Scott Cooper   *Fifteen years old. He is big for his age and handsome. He is deeply damaged. He has a vulnerability which manifests itself in cruelty. He moves and speaks with a calmness that is disarming. Sometimes he appears slow-witted. He isn't.*

Aaron Riley   *Fifteen years old. The sharper of Scott's cohorts. He and Darren dress in a similar fashion. Aaron, however, is alarmingly still. He grins a lot and hardly ever looks at the person he is speaking to. He absorbs information and language like a sponge.*

Darren Madden   *Fifteen years old. He is a simple, often bruised boy. He has the habit of spitting in thin, fine jets between his occasional comments. He is all tracksuit and jerky movements. Blunter, more monosyllabic than either Aaron and Scott and less handsome than either of them. His clothes are cheaper. He laughs quietly almost all the time.*

This play should be cast accurately to age.

The events of this play take place in the present day around the lock of the Limehouse Cut and the Lee River in East London.

The seating should be arranged in such a way as to make it possible for actors to arrive on stage from all angles, even coming from behind the sides of the audience without the audience necessarily noticing their arrival.

Several scenes in this play cut into one another. Characters from one scene will arrive on stage before the preceding scene is completed. Similarly, characters remain on stage after their own scene is completed and the following scene has begun. This should not suggest that the overlapping scenes take place in any shared 'real' time.

A Note on Punctuation
A dash (–) at the end of an incomplete sentence denotes interruption.
Ellipses (. . .) at the end of an incomplete sentence denote a trailing off.
Ellipses in place of a spoken sentence denote an inability to articulate a response.

I lie and stare at the blank ceiling, the neutral walls, the null air. God knows, adults find it hard enough to act on their knowledge of right and wrong. Can children, whose sense of right and wrong is newer but dimmer, fresher but fuzzier, act with the same clear moral sense? Do they grasp that badly hurting someone is much more wrong than stealing and truanting (which Thompson and Venables had got away with for months)? Do they have a sense of the awful irreversibility of battering a child to death with bricks? Can death have the same meaning for them as it has for an adult? I submit, your Honour, that the answer to these questions is no, no, no and no.

Blake Morrison, *As If*

But the nowness of everything is absolutely wondrous, and if people could see that, you know. There's no way of telling you, you have to experience it, but the glory of it, if you like, the comfort, the reassurance . . .The fact is, if you see the present tense, boy do you see it! And boy can you celebrate it.
Dennis Potter in interview with Melvyn Bragg, *Without Walls Special* – Channel 4, 5th April 1994

The writer would like to acknowledge the importance of the support of Graham Whybrow, Dominic Cooke, Mel Kenyon, Ian Rickson, Stephen Jeffreys and Sarah Frankcom in the writing of this play. He would like to thank the staff and pupils of Eastbrook School in Dagenham, Essex, for their constant and lasting inspiration.

Also, always, Polly Heath.

This play is dedicated to Oscar and to Dad.

SWS, March 2001

Darkness.

'Can I Pass? – instrumental' by The Rebel plays gently. After a while, and as though from some distance, we hear the sound of water. As the sound increases in volume it should become clear that it is the sound of water running through the gate of a lock. The volume of the sound increases with the volume of the water, drowning the music, and growing in time to an almost deafening level.

As the water continues a pool of blue light on the centre of the stage isolates **Billy**.

The lighting should be gentle, not allowing us a clear view of him.

He stares out to the audience for some time. In his right hand he is holding a handgun. He examines it for a moment and then briefly points it at the audience. Makes a gunshot noise with his voice and moves to throw the gun away. The lights fall on him. The noise crescendos with the fall of the lights and then quietens after a few more moments.

[************]

Light rises on the stage. It is late afternoon. Over the next five scenes the lighting will fall into evening. A path of perfectly still water runs across the front of the stage, narrowing as it runs. (See Richard Wilson's 20:50 *[1987].) There is a bench looking out over the water. When characters look out over the water they can look directly into the audience. For a short time there can still be heard the sounds of a canal.*

After a few moments, as the light rises, we should become aware of the presence of **Scott**, **Darren**, **Aaron** *and* **Adele** *on stage.* **Scott** *and* **Adele** *are in the middle of an argument. She turns away from him. He presses her.* **Darren** *is amused by* **Scott**'s *aggression and* **Adele**'s *anger.* **Aaron**, *who smokes meticulously throughout the scene, should barely pay them attention.*

Scott (*moving towards* **Adele**)   Everybody's always fucking lying about the cunt.

Aaron   She was a fucking slag.

Scott   She comes over to us, comes over to our Ross and she's giving it all this fucking eye shit. Oh Ross, she says, your eyes are so dark. She said this.

Darren   Tart.

Scott   She actually even fucking touched the boy's face. And you tell me that it's sad.

Adele   It is.

Scott   And you tell me that you miss her.

Darren   Fuck off.

Scott   That you can't stop thinking about her and I'm telling –

Adele   I can't.

Scott   I'm telling you, Del. You don't even know what you're talking about. You haven't even got a clue.

Adele   I knew her.

Scott   You didn't, Del. Not really. You never did.

Adele   She was my friend.

Scott   She was white trash.

Adele   You're lying, Scott.

Scott   Del. Fucking just shut it.

Darren   Straight up.

Scott   Thick fucking twat.

Adele (*confronting him*)   Don't talk to me like that.

Scott (*grinning, closing up on her*)   See me. When it comes to Friday. See what I'm gonna fucking do. I'm gonna come out here. I'm gonna have me a fucking party. A fucking anniversary party for her. I'm gonna toast our Ross and our Bergsie.

Adele   It didn't need to happen.

Scott   And I'm gonna toast old fucking fuckwad Charlie Russell.

Adele   They didn't need to do what they did.

Scott   And I'm gonna toast his son.

Darren   His fucking retard son.

Scott   His fucking retard son.

Adele   They deserved what they got.

Scott   And I'm gonna dance around.

He demonstrates an elegant dance movement.

Darren   Sweet.

Scott   And and and celebrate the dearly beloved fat cunt and get stoned off me dick and be happy and (*stopping dancing*) if you ever say anything like that about my brother again, Adele, I swear to Christ I'll punch you in the face so fucking hard that it'll break my fucking fist.

Aaron   Sweet as.

Scott (*becoming very still*)   Do you hear me.

Adele (*standing her ground*)   You're wrong.

Scott   Do you hear me, Adele?

Adele   I hate it when you get like this.

Scott   Do you fucking hear what I'm saying about my brother?

Adele   Yes. I hear you.

Scott   Sweet. (*He kisses her. She ignores his kiss.*) I'm going for a walk boys. You's coming?

Aaron   A fucking walk?

Scott   Yeah, man. A walk.

Darren   That'd be lovely, Scott.

Scott   Fucking get ourselves fucking sorted, eh?

Scott *moves to leave. The others follow him. And then he stops. He turns to* **Adele**.

Scott   You coming or what?

Beat.

Scott   I said. Are you coming with me or fucking what?

Adele   Yeah. Yeah, I'm coming.

She follows **Aaron** *and* **Darren** *out. As she passes* **Scott** *he strokes her back.*

Scott   Good girl.

They exit. The lights dim gently.

A moment. The sound of the water.

Billy *enters. There is an urgency about him. An eagerness. He has with him a battered school bag, and a thin bag for carrying a fishing rod. He checks that nobody is watching him and then he opens his school bag and takes out some fishing accessories. Bait, tackle, a small box of hooks, a net etc. The final object that he removes from his bag is a black, small, well kept book. A log or a diary of some sort. He opens it and presses down the correct page. He also opens up the case for his rod and fixes the two halves together. Attaches the tackle to the reel and a hook to the tackle and finally some bait. This whole process should be done quickly, with obsessive care and attention to detail. When he has finished* **Billy** *becomes completely calm. We stay with him for a short time. He makes a few notes in his book. He hums the melody from 'Can I Pass?' by The Rebel.*

Scott *enters and stands to* **Billy**'s *right. Leaning under the oak tree grinning, and drinking from a bottle of Stella Artois with remarkable speed and thirst* **Scott** *waits for some time before he speaks. He watches* **Billy** *who doesn't know that he's there.*

Scott   I thought you'd be here.

There is a pause. **Billy** *keeps calm, maybe smiles to greet* **Scott**. **Scott** *moves, slowly, towards him.*

Billy   Scott.

Scott   What are you doing?

Billy   I'm fishing.

Scott   Fishing?

Billy   For tench.

Scott (*arriving close, examining* **Billy***'s equipment*)   What are tench, Billy?

Billy   They're really small fish.

Scott   What do you do with them, Billy? When you've caught 'em?

Billy   I normally throw them back in.

Scott   What's the point of that?

Billy   It's kind of like a sport.

Scott   What's the point of throwing them back in, Billy? Waste of time, eh?

Billy   It's all to do with –

Scott (*cuts him off, about his beer*)   You want some?

Billy   No thank you.

Scott *paces around the space behind* **Billy**. **Billy** *remains fishing, but is always aware of where* **Scott** *has moved to.*

Scott (*finishes his bottle, pointing off stage*)   Did you see them little kids just up Goresbrook just now?

Billy (*enthusiastically*)   Yeah.

Scott (*puts his empty bottle in his pocket*)   I was just coming down here. I'd just been with the boys all afternoon. And I was coming down here. I was looking for you. I had something that I needed to tell you. And I saw them. They were young, eh?

Billy   Their legs are shorter.

Scott   What?

Billy   I was thinking about what it was about kids, when they're young like that, that makes them look strange. It's their legs. In comparison to the size of their heads.

Scott   Did you see what they were doing?

Billy   No.

Scott   I think they were doing bad stuff.

Billy   Oh.

Scott (*pulls out a packet of B&H*)   Sex stuff.

Billy   What?

Scott (*offers a cigarette to* **Billy**, *half knowing that he doesn't smoke*) Seriously.

Billy   No thank you.

Scott   How old do you think they were?

Billy   Twelve. Thirteen.

Scott (*lights it*)   At the oldest.

Billy   They come round here most days.

Scott   That makes me sick. Seeing that.

Billy   Are you sure that's what they were doing?

Scott   I should fucking know, Billy, eh. What do you think I am? Don't tell me you think I'm a liar, mate.

Billy   I wouldn't. I'm not. It's just. That's horrible.

Scott   Horrible?

Billy   Yeah.

Scott (*with a smoke ring*)   Do you have any brothers or sisters, Billy?

Billy   No.

Billy *reels in his line.*

Scott You wouldn't understand then, Billy, probably eh?

Billy I don't know.

Scott You wouldn't though, would you? You know about my brother, eh Billy?

Billy Yeah.

Scott But I've got a sister too. Now she's nine. If I ever heard that anybody was doing anything like that with my sister, Billy, if I ever saw my sister round here or round anywhere doing that kind of stuff I'd fucking go mental me. I'd go apeshit. I wouldn't be able to stop myself. Sometimes I get a temper on me about things like that and I end up it's like I just want to kind of fucking just go round hitting stuff.

Billy I see.

Scott She's into all kids stuff. You know like groups and that? Like Steps and shit?

Billy Yeah.

Scott She's into all that.

Billy I see.

Scott I came over cause I wanted to tell you something and I saw those kids and it just kind of did my head in a bit. (*Beat.*) Do you ever get a feeling like you're not allowed to be a child any more?

Billy What?

Scott It's just something my dad said. He said that the problem was that children aren't allowed to be children any more. I just wondered if you ever felt like that.

Billy No.

Scott No. Me neither. If I see them round here again I think that I'll tell them to fucking just go away.

Billy   They're here all the time.

Scott   Are they?

Billy (*who starts preparing a second hook*)   Normally they just throw stones at each other. Swear. Call each other fucking cunts. They draw graffiti on the walls. Write their names. Draw dicks and tits and that.

Scott (*throws his cigarette into the water*)   Good idea.

Billy (*looks up at him*)   I think they look odd. I think they look out of place. I think they look like they're shaped all wrong.

Scott   Do you?

Billy   Yeah.

Scott (*picking up and examining* **Billy**'s *fish-bait*)   You think some pretty fucked up stuff you, eh? Don't you though, Billy? You do, eh?

From here **Billy** *starts to avoid eye contact with* **Scott**. *Concentrates more on his fishing.*

Billy   What was it that you wanted to tell me?

Scott   These fish, these tench. How often do you catch them? Say, every day?

Billy   I normally catch two or three a day. At least. Sometimes much more.

Scott   Nice feeling?

Billy   When they come out of the water. They flash. They're all silvery. They look just magnificent. That's the best feeling.

The two boys take to staring out over the water. **Scott** *moves closer to* **Billy**.

Scott   Two or three a day isn't many though, Billy, is it?

Billy   It's all right.

Scott   You end up waiting a long time though, don't you?

Billy   I don't mind that. What was it that you wanted?

Scott   I've been looking for you all day. I wanted to wait until I got you on your own. I wanted to tell you. I went to see our Ross yesterday.

Billy   Did you?

Scott   It was a bit mad. You know what I mean?

Billy   I'm not sure.

Scott (*sitting with* **Billy**, **Billy** *doesn't acknowledge him*)   He's changed. He seems quite quiet.

Billy   I see.

Scott   It was fucking horrible, Billy. I can't stop thinking about it. It actually made me want to throw up. Ross told me, and this is what I'm here for, Billy, Ross told me to say hello to your dad.

Billy *says nothing.*

Scott   And I probably won't see him. I don't see your dad that much. And when I do he kind of avoids me.

Billy   I see.

Scott   Billy, tell him he's asking after him.

Billy   Right.

Scott   Checking that he's all right and that. Looking forward to seeing him soon. He'll be thinking about him Friday Billy. It is very important that you pass this message on, Billy, you with me?

Billy   Yeah.

Scott   Are you sure?

Billy   Yes.

Scott   Because you fucking better be.

Billy   I am.

Scott (*ruffles* **Billy***'s hair,* **Billy** *doesn't move*)   How is your dad, Billy?

Billy   He's all right.

Scott   Good. I mean after everything that happened.

Billy   He sleeps a lot.

Scott   Right. Well that probably helps I reckon, eh Billy? (*No response.*) I would imagine that plenty of sleep is exactly what he needs even. To replenish himself. You know what I mean, Bill? (*No response. Pause. Grinning.*) I should be going, Billy. I'll probably come back later. See how you're doing and that. Maybe bring some of the boys with us if that's all right with you, yeah? (*Beat.* **Scott** *stands.*) Billy.

Billy   Yeah.

Scott   Were you lying about your brothers and sisters?

Billy (*turns to him*)   What?

Scott (*with a big smile*)   Good man. Laters, eh?

Scott *exits.* **Billy** *turns to look away into the opposite direction from where* **Scott** *leaves. He reels in his hook and sits back on his heels for a short time. The lights are dimming gently.* **Billy** *is trying to calm himself, rocking back and forth on his heels. He is unsure what action needs to be taken but he understands that something must be done. He stands after a short time and exits right.*

Lights dim faintly and rise a little again.

Charlie *enters. He sits looking out over the water.*

Billy *enters left after a few minutes and watches him.* **Charlie** *talks to* **Billy** *without looking at him.*

Charlie   One time. I come down here. There was a heron. Perched. Just resting. You know up by Goresbrook House?

Billy   Where have you been, Dad? I've been looking for you for ages.

Charlie (*grins*)   Just resting. Just there like. Sitting. Beautiful it was. It had these white feathers. And you look closely you can see these feathers just getting touched by the wind. Gorgeous black eyes it had. And still like nothing you'd ever see. I come down here. Watched it. And you wait two seconds and the cunt just swoops. Drops like a lead ball. The weight of it. Plunges down. Comes up in a second with a carp in its beak, Billy. Honestly. It was one of the most breathtaking sights that I ever saw.

Billy   How long have you been here?

Charlie   So I come back. Two days later. Bring a gun with me, don't I? Wait to shoot the bastard. I was going to shoot it. Blow its head off and stick it on the wall at home. Buy one of those little wooden plaques. One of those things. Just glue it up there. Waiting two days. Cunts fucked off 'a'n' it? Never comes back.

Billy   How long have you been here, Dad?

Charlie   Not long, Billy, don't worry.

Billy *moves to sit with his father. He fidgets while his father speaks.*

Charlie   I remember when I bought the bastard. Lewis Matthews. Geezer who sold it to us. I told him that I wanted it to shoot the herons that were eating my fish and also for protection from robbers and that and he says to me, he said, 'Charlie,' he said. 'Don't ever leave it around unloaded.' Which surprised me. At the time. He said, ''cause one day you're going to fucking want to shoot the cunt. You'll fucking wake up and some cunt'll be fucking robbing you. So always put a fucking bullet in it. Four chambers round the barrel and it's one two three four BANG!' (*Pause.*) Sometimes I just take it out. Think about all the people I could shoot. Y'know what I mean?

Billy   Dad, I've got to tell you something.

Charlie   I've been waiting for you, Billy.

Billy   Dad, something's happened.

Charlie   You get out late, did you?

Billy   Dad –

Charlie   Fucking detention again, was it? You been mouthing off again probably, have you?

Billy   Dad, just listen to us for a minute, will ya?

Charlie (*containing his violence*)   You're not fucking trying one over on me, are you, Billy? Because I'm fucking warning you . . .

Beat. **Billy** *decides to wait for a while.*

Billy   Course I'm not. I've been looking for you.

Charlie *starts fishing with the equipment that* **Billy** *left from the last scene.*

Charlie   Well, I've been here. What was it you needed to tell us?

Billy   It can wait.

Billy *sits with his father. Some time.*

Billy   Did you get out today?

Charlie   Yeah.

Billy   Did ya?

Charlie   I'm out now, ain't I?

Billy   Did you go down the dole?

Charlie   Yeah.

Billy   And did you tell 'em about the water bill?

Charlie   Yes.

Billy   'Cause we don't need to pay that. They shouldn't even be sending us that.

Charlie   I told 'em.

Billy   Was there anything going? Any jobs, was there?

Charlie   I didn't get a chance to have a look.

Billy   You what?

Charlie   I didn't have time.

Billy   What do you mean you didn't have time? What takes up your time, Dad? What have you been doing all day?

Charlie   Billy, son, just fucking, just give it a break, will you?

Billy   Honestly, Dad, you can't even sort it out to go and have a look at the notice boards in the dole while you're actually in there even, you're actually in the actual office, Dad. You do my head in sometimes. You do. (*Beat. Collecting it from his pocket.*) Here. My report. You've got to sign this.

Charlie   What's this?

Billy   It's my punctuality report, Dad. I've told you about this.

Charlie   What do you need a punctuality report for, Billy? What the fuck's wrong with your punctuality?

Billy   Everybody gets them if they're a little late a couple of times. I wanted to be on it.

Charlie   You what?

Billy   I wanted to be on it because I was getting a bit worried.

Charlie   Well if you were getting a bit worried, Billy, if you were getting a bit worried, mate, what were you being so late for, eh?

Billy   I don't know, Dad, honest. It's not that big a deal. I told you this. Here. You've got to read it. And sign it. They need it.

Charlie (*reading*)   'Excellent. Excellent. Very good behaviour. Very good, if a little quiet.' Who's that? Biology.

Billy   Mr Warren.

Charlie (*putting out his cigarette*)   What's he fucking going on about? 'If a little quiet.' He should be fucking glad is what he should fucking be. Dickhead. (*Beat.*) 'Good. Very good. Very good day, Billy.' Well fuck me. Billy, this is a fucking bleeding miracle is what this is. I need to sign this then, do I?

Billy   At the bottom. They need it.

Charlie *pulls a pen from his pocket and signs the report. Hands it back.* **Billy** *takes it, smiling, folds it neatly and goes to put it back in his bag.*

Charlie   Who needs it?

Billy   The school. They need to keep a track on me. It's important.

Charlie   Right.

Billy   For the records.

Charlie   Right.

Billy   'Cause, because if we, if we move and I go to another school then they're going to need all this information so they can send it on to my new school. Dad.

Charlie   Billy just don't . . . best not lose it then, eh?

Billy   I won't. I'll give it back to him tomorrow.

Beat.

Billy   Dad.

Charlie   Billy.

Billy   Can I ask you a question.

Charlie   Go on.

Billy   Have you changed your shirt?

Charlie   You what?

Billy   Have you?

Charlie   . . .

Billy   You haven't, have you?

Charlie   I . . .

Billy   You've got to change your shirts, Dad.

Charlie   Jesus fucking Christ on a bike.

Billy   I even, didn't I, I even just washed 'em for you. I even just left one out for you.

Charlie   Will you give it a rest?

Billy   What's going to happen, Dad, say they have to have an interview, say somebody comes and they're trying to sort out a new flat for us or they're checking up on us or that . . .

Charlie   Billy.

Billy   Say they are though.

Charlie   I don't think that's going to happen, son.

Billy   It might do. Say they do. And you're there. And you're looking like a right tramp. I really worry about it. Sometimes. I really do.

Charlie   Well fucking don't.

Billy   Well I can't help it.

Charlie   Well try.

Billy   Dad. I saw Scott Cooper.

Charlie   Did you?

Billy   Yeah. He told me to tell you something. He told me to tell you that he'd been to see his Ross.

Charlie   Right. (*Beat.*) I see. (*Another.*) Billy.

Billy   Yeah.

Charlie   Is that what this is all about?

Billy   All what's about?

Charlie   All fucking this palaver. Billy, do I look like a twat?

Billy   What?

Charlie   Do I look like a fucking twat, Billy? You heard me.

Billy   No.

Charlie   No. Of course I fucking don't. I'm a handsome bastard me and I'm not a fucking stupid twat. So why do you think, Billy, thinking about it and everything, why do you think I should even, even for the slightest moment even, why should I even care what that prick Scott Cooper has fucking been up to with his spare time? Eh, Billy? Answer me that one, pal.

Billy   Dad, he's been to see his Ross.

Charlie   I don't care.

Billy   And his Ross had told him that he was thinking about you.

Charlie   Billy, I couldn't give a monkey's fuck.

Billy   Dad, I think I'm scared.

Charlie   What?

Billy   I think I'm scared of what's going to happen when they get out.

Charlie   Oh fucking listen to it, will ya?

Billy   Dad.

Charlie   Listen to it fucking going on! Jesus fucking H. Billy, you're worse than your fucking mother!

Billy   Dad, don't.

Charlie   Billy, son. I don't give a shite. I don't give a shite what Scott Cooper has been doing. I don't give a shite about what his retard fucking brother's been saying. And you tell me that you're scared.

Billy   I am.

Charlie   Well, Billy, I promise you, son. You have fucking nothing to be scared of, mate. Fucking nothing. You hear me? Do you?

Billy   Yeah.

Charlie   Fucking . . . good. You better. So just fucking quit it, all right?

Pause.

Billy   Dad.

Charlie (*treads his cigarette out*)   Billy.

Billy   I saw Mum yesterday.

Charlie (*turning to look*)   Where?

Billy   Down the market.

Charlie   What were you doing down the market yesterday?

Billy   After school.

Charlie   Did she see you?

Billy   I don't know. I don't think so.

Charlie (*looks to* **Billy***, concerned*)   Did she speak to you?

Billy   No.

Charlie *watches* **Billy**. **Billy**, *not sure how his Dad will react, finds it difficult to hold his stare.* **Michelle** *enters. Neither* **Charlie** *nor* **Billy** *acknowledges her. It is* **Billy** *who breaks the tension between the two.*

Billy   Dad, I think if we're going to leave here, Dad. I think we should think about going soon.

Charlie *watches* **Billy** *for a short time. He never says what he is thinking. Instead he hands him some money.*

Charlie   Get yourself some chips. I want you home by ten o'clock.

Billy   Right.

Charlie   Ten o'clock, Billy. I want you back home.

Billy   Dad, do you know what day it is on Friday?

Pause. **Charlie** *glares at* **Billy** *and then breaks the tension with some reluctance.*

Charlie   Don't be late. I'll see you later.

He turns and leaves. Exchanges a long glance with **Michelle** *as he exits.* **Billy** *watches him go.*

Billy *turns to look at* **Michelle**. *The lights should dim, almost imperceptibly.*

Michelle   Hello, Billy. How are you, darling?

Very long pause. She buttons her coat up.

Billy   There's something I've got to tell you, Mum, it's very important.

Michelle   I thought it was you. The other day and that. Up on Roman Road. I thought, I thought it was you.

Billy   Mum.

Michelle   You've grown, you know? Billy? You've really grown. And filled out like. In your shoulders and that. Billy. Billy, you look lovely you know.

Billy   Mum, do you know somebody called Scott Cooper?

Michelle   Scott who?

Billy   Scott Cooper, Mum, he's a boy from down Goresbrook?

Michelle   No, Billy, I've never heard of him.

Billy   Well –

Michelle (*cuts him off*)   How's school? Billy?

Nervously, half shaking, she lights a cigarette.

Billy   You've got to tell something to Danny and Leanne.

Michelle   And how's, how's, how's Charlie? Are you all right? Are you eating all right? The pair of you?

Billy   Yes, Mum, we're fine.

Michelle   And are you staying out of trouble? Out of bother with your teachers? And doing your homework?

Billy   You've got to tell Danny and Leanne that if they come across a boy called Scott Cooper that they mustn't, they, they mustn't talk to him or look at him or listen to him or anything. They've got to, it's very important that they've got to just leave him alone. Are you with me, Mum?

Michelle   Of course I am, Billy.

Billy   Will you tell them?

Michelle   Of course I will, Billy.

Billy (*making to leave*)   If Dad knew I was talking to you he'd do his nut I swear.

Michelle (*stopping him*)   Billy. Don't go. Just not yet.

He turns. She moves towards him, slowly, cautiously. As soon as she makes the slightest movement to touch him he explodes at her.

Billy   Don't touch me.

She freezes, pulls back and leaves.

He turns away from her and begins to pack away his fishing equipment. He packs furiously and chaotically. Interrupting his packing by writing occasional phrases or sentences in his book.

Adele *enters. She stands some distance away from* **Billy** *and from where he is packing and writing. She waits. She spends some moments staring out over the water before she turns to watch* **Billy***. When she speaks he stops his packing for a short time. But only for a short time.*

Adele   You're Billy. Billy Russell. You go to our school. (*No response.*) You're in Mr Webster's form. 4D. I hate him. He's a fat cunt. (*No response.*) You live on the Cotall Street Estate. Up Limehouse. Opposite Stainsby Road, your flat is. I've seen you. Not only at school and that. I live just near you. I'm not being a funny cow. Honestly. I've just noticed you. I'm Adele.

Billy   I know.

Adele   What you doing?

Billy (*who continues to pack up*)   I was fishing.

Adele (*approaches him*)   You're always fishing, aren't you? Heh? Every day I come here you're here fishing. With your dad normally. Where's your dad today, Billy? (*No response. He continues to pack.*) Don't you want to talk to us? It's all right. I'm not going to bite you or nothing. It's a bit fucking weird though. Don't you think, Billy?

Billy   No.

Billy*, packed up, carrying only his book separately, goes to leave.*

Adele   Where are you going?

Billy (*stops*)   Home.

Adele (*taking the piss*)   What are you running away from, Billy? What are you trying to escape from?

Billy   Can I ask you something?

Adele   It speaks!

Billy   Can I?

Adele   Go on.

Billy   You come down this way, every day. At, at the same time every day. Exact same time. And you stop. Just for a second and that. But you do, you just, you stop. At the same point. Just looking up there. Out there across the other side. And then you carry on. Can I ask you?

Adele   What?

Billy   Why do you do that?

Adele   It's none of your business.

Billy   No. I know that. I just thought I'd ask you. I'm sorry. I'm just inquisitive. I'm a strange fucker sometimes. (*Pause.*) Is it . . . ?

Adele   What?

Billy   Is it because of Racheal?

There is a moment between the two. And then **Adele** *grins.*

Adele   You know something I noticed. (*No response.*) You're going to think this is well weird.

Billy   What?

Adele   You've got the same eyes as your dad.

Billy   That's not true.

Adele   Yeah, it is. Was it your dad who found her?

Billy   What?

Adele   Racheal. Was it your dad who found her?

Long pause.

Billy   Yes. It was.

Adele   That's what I heard. Did you see her too?

Billy   No.

Adele   What was it like?

Billy   What do you mean?

Adele   Did he never say, your dad, what it was like? What happened? How come he found her? Anything like that?

Billy   No.

Adele   Did you never ask him?

Billy   No.

Adele   'Cause I would have. I would never have shut up about it. It was Ross Cooper, wasn't it? And Berg Kempton. And his mates? Who did it?

Billy   Yeah.

Adele   Your dad saw 'em, didn't he?

Long silence.

Did you know her?

Billy   Not really.

Adele (**Billy** *turns to her as she speaks*)   I used to sit with her in English. She was very quiet. She was quite, you know, she was like quite fat and that. Never said anything but sometimes, if you were working in pairs and that, she used to know so much stuff. She used to talk about why people did things. She had all these ideas. Never told them to anybody. Except she'd tell them to me, though, and I'd tell the teacher and he'd think I was a right boffin. But it was all her.

Billy   I'm not in your year. I'm in Year Ten.

Adele   I know. (*New tactic. She moves towards him.*) I remember when you arrived at our school. You only came a couple of years back, didn't you?

Billy (*keeps his ground*)   Yeah.

Adele   Where did you go before?

Billy   Morpeth.

Adele   Did you? (*No response.*) How come you changed?

Billy (*looking away*)   We moved.

Adele   To Cotall Street?

Billy   That's right.

Adele   How come?

Billy (*turning back to her*)   Aren't you Scott Cooper's girlfriend?

Adele   No.

Billy   That's not what I heard.

Adele   I'm not.

Billy   Isn't he going to be a bit fucked off that you're coming round here talking to me?

Adele   I'm not his girlfriend. How come you moved?

Billy (*moving to collect his fishing bag*)   If I know Scott Cooper he'll be fucking angry and he'll probably most likely fucking want to batter the pair of us.

Adele   Scott Cooper's a needledick.

Billy   But he'll still fucking batter us.

Adele   How come you moved?

Billy   I came to live with me dad. I used to live with me mum.

Adele   How come you changed?

No response. **Billy** *looks away from her.*

Adele   You know what your problem is? Billy, don't you? You're just fucking plain rude sometimes. It's no wonder you've got no mates.

No response.

And I'm trying to be dead friendly. And you just ignore us.

Billy (*explaining*)   I was leaving school one time last week.
There was a lad waiting outside the school. An older lad.
About eighteen. I watch him waiting at the bus stop. And
he's waiting for a kid in Year Ten.

Billy *turns to confront her with his justification. She doesn't break eye
contact with him.*

Billy   As I'm coming out of the gates the kid in Year Ten
is walking ahead of me and this lad gets him. This eighteen-
year-old. Gets him. Gets him by his coat. And he pulls his
head down and smacks it against a lamp-post. Four times.
Back and down against the metal bit on the lamp-post.

Adele   So?

Billy   I've seen teachers talk to kids as though they are
worthless scabby shit. Bully them. Humiliate them. Never
think about stopping and asking if they need help but
instead, they just, instead they just say stupid cruel things.
And the reason they do it is because so many of the kids, not
all of them, but so fucking many are so fucking stupid and
dick around and act like tossers. They think it's funny. It's
not. It's shitty. And it ruins things.

Adele   What the fuck has that got to do with anything?

Billy   I come down here, Adele Kent, and there is litter,
pissy fucked litter everywhere. And it's kids that have
left it.

Adele   Billy.

Billy   Even here. Even the surface of the water. The place
looks like it's fucking ripped up. People don't care. Do they?
Even about trees and that? People just, why do they, just
fucking, the way people treat trees around here is
despicable!

Adele   What has that got to do with anything?

Billy (*concluding*)   It's not just me.

Adele   That's not an excuse.

Billy   What do you want?

Adele   How did you know my surname?

Billy   I found it out. I asked somebody. What do you want?

Adele   Why did you do that?

Billy   Because I wanted to know. What do you want from me, Adele?

Adele   I found out about your dad. And I thought it was interesting. I wanted to meet you.

Billy   It isn't.

Adele   What?

Billy   Interesting.

Adele (*proving him wrong*)   When I was four my mum was put into mental hospital because she tried to kill herself. I only found that out just this year. My dad's psychic. He's got psychic powers. He can see people's souls. What they look like. I don't know if I like him or not. Parents are *always* interesting.

Billy   That's not true.

Adele   Parents are always interesting. Because they're always fucked but they're very close to how you are yourself. You do things and it's just the same as them.

Billy   I'm nothing like my dad.

Adele (*ignoring him*)   So when I heard about Charlie I thought that the easiest way to find out about what happened, about him, was to find out about you.

Billy   I'm nothing like my dad.

Adele   I bet you are. (*No response.*) I used to know Berg Kempton. My mum used to work in their pub up Ilford. She used to be a cleaner. They used to come down Cotall Street. I saw him once get a baseball bat and smack this kid's arm up. The kid was, what, fifteen. How long's he gone down for?

Billy   Ten years.

Adele   When he comes out do you think he's going to look for your dad?

Billy   I don't know.

Pause.

Adele   It was this time last year, wasn't it? (*No response.*) Billy. It was a year ago on Friday. You remember? (*No response.*) It was horrible, Billy, wasn't it?

Billy   Yeah.

Adele   There was six of them, I heard, wasn't there?

Billy   Yeah.

Adele   What do you think she thought? When she saw them?

Billy   I don't know.

Adele   You never can know, Billy, can you?

Billy   . . .

Adele   You wanna know something?

Billy   What?

Adele   I'm on seven different types of medication.

Billy   You what?

Adele   I take two different types of pills for epilepsy. I've had fits. Two fits. Not for years.

Billy   So what do you want me to do about it?

Adele   And I have nightmares.

Billy   What?

Adele   I think it's almost funny sometimes. I've seen people, people I know take speed, pills, draw, gas, booze, charlie, glue, smack. I've seen people smoking smack outside my flat, Billy, on our estate. Right in front of the Old Bill.

Billy   So what are you telling me this for?

Adele (*moving towards him*)   Sometimes at night I still get frightened. Of the streets near where I live. Of the gangs there. The junkies. The scumfuckers. The scuzzbags. The perverts.

Billy   What are you going on about, you?

Adele   I just wanted to meet somebody. To talk to somebody. Somebody who knew her. I wanted to meet you, Billy. To see if you were all right. Billy, I think about her all the time.

Long pause. They should be quite close by now.

Billy   You know who frightens me?

Adele   Who?

Scott *has entered with* **Aaron** *and* **Darren**. *The three boys drink beer. Smoke cigarettes. They surround* **Billy** *and* **Adele**, *but remain around the peripheries of the stage for now, allowing them to continue uninterrupted.*

Billy   All the winos and that. The boozers. When you walk past them, you never know if they're going to smack out or what.

Adele   No, you don't.

Billy   I have this theory about what happens to you when you're dead.

Adele   Oh yeah?

Billy   I think when you're dead you go up to heaven and you meet God and he asks you if you think that, after the things that you have done in your lifetime, you deserve to go to heaven or to hell. And you have to answer. And the answer decides where you go but you have to be completely absolutely honest about it. And there's nothing worse than lying in this test. Because God can, he can just fucking well tell, can't he. And if you lie, well, you're really fucked. And those winos, all those, those people. They're fucked too. I think.

Adele (*bewildered*)   That's about the stupidest idea I've ever heard.

Billy   Where do you think you'll go?

Adele (*still bewildered*)   Jesus.

Billy   Where do you think Racheal will be?

Adele (*serious*)   I don't believe in heaven. Or hell.

There is a slight moment. **Adele** *and the boys ignore each other when* **Scott** *starts to speak.*

Scott   We was just thinking about you.

Billy   What?

Scott *removes a cigarette from his packet. Leaves it unlit for now, occasionally dangling between his teeth.*

Scott   We were having a conversation. About Bergsie. Ross. And that. And the conversation kind of came around to you.

Billy   Right.

Scott   Which might surprise you. But might not. I was gonna ask you a question.

Adele *touches* **Billy**'s *face. Leaves. Takes a swig from* **Scott**'s *bottle as she goes. Nobody, however, pays any attention as she leaves. The lights fall to nighttime.*

Billy   Go on.

Scott   You moved schools, yeah?

Billy   Yeah.

Scott   We couldn't remember. We couldn't figure it out.

Aaron   Remember I think is fairer, Scott.

Scott   Yeah. Fair enough. We couldn't remember. Why did you move schools, Billy?

Billy   Moved house.

Darren   Makes sense.

Aaron   Although it is a little evasive.

Scott   Yes. You moved house. Why?

Billy   What?

Scott   Why did you move house?

Billy   I went to live with me dad.

Scott (*moves in*)   What was wrong with your mum?

Billy   Nothing.

Aaron (*moves in*)   Well if there was nothing wrong with her, Billy, then how come you fucking fucked off and left her, boy?

Billy   Just did, that's all.

Scott   And your brother and your sister?

Billy   I haven't got a brother and a sister.

Scott (*strikes a match*)   Liar.

Billy   What?

Scott (*lights his cigarette*)   Isn't he, lads? He's a fucking liar.

Darren (*moves in, with a big swig from his bottle*)   He's a fucking dick.

Scott   I mean, it's not a big deal. But to deny your own brother, Billy, your own sister. I think that's a little out of order. Don't you, boys?

Aaron   I think it's fucking abject!

Scott   Mind you, boys, have you seen his mum?

Darren   What?

Scott   Billy's mum. Have you seen her?

Darren   Nah.

Scott   Straight up, man, she is fucking tight.

Darren   Right!

Scott   Ain't it, Billy? Don't you think, I mean, I know you're not meant to think stuff like this but your mum, Billy, even you can see that she is one straight up fucking sweet bit of pussy, yeah?

Billy   Why are you talking as though you're American?

Some time. Some tension. **Scott***'s cigarette close up to* **Billy***'s unflinching face.*

Scott   Billy.

Billy   What?

Scott   Billy.

Billy   What?

Scott   Billy.

Billy   What?

Scott   Shut your mouth or I'll cut your eyes out.

Darren (*finishes his beer in celebration*)   Damn straight, Scott.

Scott   Billy's mum's got a sweet little pussy though, Billy, ain't it?

Darren   What are her titties like, Scott?

Scott   Fucking I never saw her titties, man.

Darren   Nah?

Scott   Nah, I fucked her with my eyes closed.

Darren   Sweet.

Scott   Tight little cunt but, to tell you the truth, Billy, eh? Her face is a mushy pile of shit.

Darren   You know what I heard about his mum, Scott? I heard his mum works hard.

Scott   Damn hard.

Darren   Works all night sometimes.

Aaron   I seen her. But I spent my money elsewhere. Because I figured she's a fucking filthy cunt. With lice. Crabs. All manner of venereal disease.

Darren (*swigs from* **Aaron***'s bottle*)   AIDS.

Scott   Billy, has your mum got AIDS?

Aaron (*wipes bottle neck*)   Did she get it from fucking monkeys, Billy, 'cause I heard she's hungry for monkey cock? Although that's an unsubstantiated rumour.

Darren   Billy's mum's got AIDS big time.

Aaron (*lights a cigarette*)   Billy, do you ever think about what it would be like to fuck your Mum? Do you ever think about that? 'Cause if you ever do, just ask Scott, and I'm sure he'll tell you. (*Hacking cough / laugh.*)

Darren   He's told us enough times.

Billy   Shut up.

Darren (*claps / rubs his hands*)   Ooooohhhhh!

Aaron (*in a fake scientist's voice*)   I do believe that this peculiar worm is turning, Scott.

Scott (*threatening, quiet*)   I can see. (*Beat.*) Boys. (*Another. Release.*) Lay off, eh? We're just joking, Billy. Just pissing you about. No offence, eh? Billy? No offence? Is it? Boys? Billy?

You're not offended, are you, Billy? We're sorry, aren't we boys?

Aaron Yeah. Right.

Scott (*perhaps ruffles his hair*) Billy. You need to chill, man. I mean I'm not saying anything but you're a bit of an uptight cunt, Billy, sometimes. You need to learn to take a bit of a joke, you with me, Billy? (*Beat.*) Billy. Have you got any money?

Billy What?

Scott Have you got any money for us?

Billy I've got one quid fifty.

Scott That's fine, Billy.

Billy What?

Scott Just give us your one quid fifty then, if that's all you've got.

Billy I need it.

Scott I'm sorry?

Billy It's my chip money.

Darren You need it?

Billy I . . .

Aaron I'm a little surprised by that comment, frankly.

Billy I need the money for my tea.

Scott (*not menacing*) Just give it to us, Billy, would ya? Stop confusing the issue with irrelevant fucking horseshit.

Billy *hands over the money. He starts to move away from them.*

Billy I won't be able to get my chips now.

Scott I'm sorry?

Darren Billy, we've got to eat too, man, y'know?

Aaron   Selfish bastard.

Scott   How's your dad, Billy?

Billy *stops.*

Darren   I was speaking to Bergsie's brother.

Aaron   Fucking hell. He is certainly not happy.

Scott   Year ago this week, innit?

Aaron   Friday.

Darren   Apparently Bergsie's had to tell his brother not to go near your dad or nothing because he wants to cut him himself when he comes out.

Scott   No shit?

Darren   That's what he said.

Scott   Won't be long now, will it? Good behaviour and that. Couple of years maybe.

Darren   If that.

Aaron   Billy, I heard something about your dad.

Darren   I heard lots of things about his dad.

Aaron   Is it true that your dad likes a nice pull.

Darren   `A nice what?

Aaron   A nice pull. A nice wank. A nice little shuffle.

Scott   Don't we all, Riley, eh? That's not a crime.

Darren   Fucking hope not.

Aaron   Yeah. But a nice quiet pull when he's fishing.

Scott   What?

Aaron   Gets it out in public.

Scott   No?

Aaron   No shit. My sister saw him.

Darren   Fuck off!

Aaron   He grinned at her and everything.

Darren   Just where Racheal was and that.

Scott (*treads his cigarette out*)   You think he's thinking about it?

Darren   Damn right he is. Wanking himself off, thinking about Racheal.

Aaron   Thinking about pulling her body up again.

Scott   Thinking about what he saw!

Aaron   Sick fuck.

Darren   Sick fucking cunt, I think.

Scott (*closing in on* **Billy**, *pronounces every consonant*)   You know that, Billy? Your dad is a sick fucking cunt and when Bergsie cuts him, and when our Ross fucking stabs him there are going to be many more people who are happy than there are who are sad. Because he's a cunt. And a grass. And a pervert.

Billy (*turning to confront them*)   That's not true.

Scott   You what?

Billy   That isn't true.

Scott   What isn't true, Billy?

Billy   Anything that you said. About my mum. Or about my dad. It's not true.

Scott   Are you questioning me?

Darren (*quietly*)   Fucksake!

Aaron (*concerned*)   Billy, man, don't!

Scott   Billy, are you questioning me?

Billy   It isn't true.

Scott   Don't be fucking questioning me, Billy. Really. Don't fucking do that. FUCK!

He explodes at him and knocks him back slightly. Clasps his face between his hands.

Scott   'Cause I'm not pissing you, Billy. I'm not fucking joking, son. If you ever fucking so much as ever fucking question me, talk to me. To me, like that. Touch fucking ME! Like that. Again. I swear to Christ, Billy, I will cut your tiny dick off. You understand me, Billy?

Billy   I didn't touch you.

Scott   Do you understand me?

Billy   Yes. I do.

Darren *and* **Aaron** *watch as* **Scott** *stares at* **Billy** *for some time, still holding his face.*

'Can I Pass? – instrumental' by The Rebel plays as the lights fall to darkness for a while.

Lights rise. It is early afternoon. **Billy** *and* **Charlie** *are together on stage, facing out towards the audience. They are fishing. There is a long pause as they fish. As they fish* **Billy** *occasionally looks to his dad, as though waiting for the right time to speak. When he answers his dad's questions he seems more detached than we have seen him before.*

Charlie   Keep calm. Don't move unless it is absolutely necessary. Keep still. Stay absolutely steady. Watch the details of the water. They'll come eventually. (*Pause.*) How was school?

Billy   It was all right.

Charlie   You done your homework?

Billy   Yeah.

Charlie   All of it?

Billy   Yeah.

Charlie   Already?

Billy   Yeah.

Charlie   Properly?

Billy   Yeah.

Charlie   I bet you fucking ain't. I bet you fucked it all up, knowing you, probably.

Billy   I never.

Charlie   Well, they don't fucking give you much, do they?

Billy   No.

Charlie   Probably don't like fucking marking it all, heh?

Billy   Probably.

Charlie   Lazy tarts. Probably just like want a fucking afternoon off. Probably. (*Beat.*) You staying out of bother?

Billy   Yeah.

Charlie   Are you?

Billy   Yeah.

Charlie   You better had be.

Billy   I am.

Charlie   'Cause I don't want to find out about you doing all kinds of mad stuff again, Billy.

Billy   You won't.

Charlie   I don't want you getting in with any bad old bastards.

Billy   I won't.

Charlie   You better not be.

Billy   I won't.

Charlie   I'm warning you.

Billy   I'm not. (*Beat.*) Dad, have I got your eyes?

Charlie   What do you mean?

Billy   It's just something somebody said to me.

Charlie   I hate it when people say all that shit. I can never figure it out. You've got your own eyes.

Billy   People have said it before though, eh? I remember even Mum used to say I had your eyes.

Pause. Tension for a short while.

Charlie   See, you know what your fucking problem is, don't ya? You're up with the fucking fairies half the fucking time. You're away with the fucking stars. Cloud fucking cuckoo land, Billy, isn't it? Got a head like a fucking Teletubby sometimes, Billy, honestly.

Billy   I got cut today.

Charlie   You what?

Billy   Today. At school. I got cut.

Charlie   On what?

Billy   On a fishing hook.

Charlie   On a what?

Billy   A fishing hook.

Charlie   How the fuck did you get cut on a fucking fishing hook?

Billy   I took a little box of fishing hooks up to the school to show our teacher and I was fiddling about with one of them in science and it went right through my thumb. I had to pull it out. Tore the skin right off my thumb and all. I thought I'd better tell ya.

Charlie   You fucking stupid bastard.

Billy   I thought I better tell you, Dad, because I didn't want you to get mad or anything.

Charlie   Billy for crying out loud.

Billy   You should have seen Mr Thompson. He nearly puked up. And the woman in the office, the secretary who does all of the injuries and the sick notes and that. She was looking at it going 'Oh Billy! What are we going to do?' I said, 'I could just pull it out, Miss.' She wasn't sure what to do, so I did. I just pulled it out. Blood spitting all over the place. It was funny. Made me laugh.

Charlie   Billy, what the fuck is the matter with you?

Billy   Some people get a bit sick around the sight of blood but it never really bothers me too much.

Charlie   Billy, you can't take fucking fishing hooks into school with you, you daft twat.

Billy   I wanted to show Mr Thompson what they looked like.

Charlie   I don't care.

Billy   He'd been asking about them.

Charlie   Billy.

Billy   What?

Charlie   I'll tell you something for nothing, son.

Billy   What?

Charlie   If I hear you've been fucking about with fishing hooks or shit like that again, at school or fucking anywhere, I'll take 'em fucking off you, so help me God I will, and I will stick 'em up your fucking arse.

Billy *never even looks at him.*

Billy   Right.

Charlie   For fucksake. I've told you.

Billy   What?

Charlie   Haven't I? About why this is important. Billy. Haven't I told you?

Billy   Yeah.

Charlie   You have just got to be, just you've got to be just bang on, Billy.

Billy   I know.

Charlie   Just absolutely bang on, mate.

Billy   You've told me that, Dad.

Charlie   I don't want no cunt from anywhere coming round here and saying that you're not, that you are not allowed to stay here any more. Billy. That you're not allowed to stay with me. And if you fuck up. If you fuck up, Billy, they will. They told us that. They'll come, Billy, they'll come and they will take you. You know that, don't you?

Billy   Yeah.

Charlie   So, just, fucking be good.

Billy   I try.

Charlie   You what?

Billy   I said I try. To be good. I really do.

Charlie   Well try fucking harder.

Billy   Dad.

Charlie   Billy.

Billy   Can I ask you a question?

Charlie   Fucking hell, Billy, what are you like? What is it with all these fucking questions? I feel like I'm on fucking Wogan.

Billy   Can I?

Charlie   Go on.

Billy   It's a bit strange.

Charlie   All right.

Billy   Dad. When you, when you found Racheal, Dad, what was it like?

Pause.

Charlie   Why?

Billy   What?

Charlie   Why do you want to know?

Billy   Because I think about it all the time.

Charlie   It was a long time ago, Billy.

Billy   Dad, it was a year ago. It's not that long.

Charlie   I don't remember much about it, Billy. I try not to think about it.

Charlie *reels in his line, removes the bait from the hook.*

Billy   Dad, did you see them get her? Ross and Bergsie? Did you see them?

No response.

Billy   Ross's brother reckons you saw them and that you phoned the police. Is that true?

No response.

Billy   Dad, are you scared about what's going to happen when Bergsie gets out? Because I am. I think we should think about going, Dad.

Charlie   Billy, I've told you. I'm waiting.

Billy   I don't think it makes any sense waiting, Dad.

Charlie   Billy.

Billy   Dad, Ross's brother reckons that when Bergsie gets out that he's going to try and stab you. And I believe him, Dad. I honestly do.

Charlie *removes his line and packs up his rod. Stands to leave.*
Adele *enters quietly and lies down staring at the sky.*

Charlie   He won't.

Billy   Dad, I really think that he's going to try.

Charlie   He won't. He won't be out for ten years, Billy. We won't be here then.

Adele   When it gets as hot as this I can't even think.

Charlie *leaves.* **Billy** *watches him go. He opens his book and writes. He continues to write while* **Adele** *talks to him. The lights should brighten and become warmer throughout this scene.*

Billy   I like it.

Adele   I feel like I'm trapped in a cupboard. They shouldn't make us go to school when it's as hot as this. They shouldn't make us do anything. Nothing.

Billy   I find that it clears my head.

Adele   And the teachers get pissed off. Treat you like wasps. (*Beat.*) Has Scott spoken to you?

Billy   I watch all of the people who come down here. On their way somewhere.

Adele   Has he, Billy?

Billy   No. Nobody ever stops.

Adele   'Cause he told me he was going to.

Billy   Well he hasn't.

Adele   Good. I was worried that he would find you.

Billy   Do you remember when you were little how aeroplanes sounded?

Adele (*propping herself up*)   What?

Billy   Did you ever lie on your back and look up at the sky and watch the aeroplanes fly over your head and listen to the sound that they made?

Adele   All the time.

Billy   As they get older, people just don't notice things like that.

Adele   They don't get time.

Pause. **Billy** *gets up, starts to reel in his line and remove the bait and the hook.*

Adele (*considered*)   Sometimes I wish I could still be in primary school. I used to love it there.

Billy   There's no point wasting time thinking about things that have finished, Adele. You have to, I have to, I look forward to stuff all the time.

Adele   What do you look forward to?

Billy   Going away. We're going away. Me and our dad. We're going to leave here and go down and live by the sea.

Adele   When?

Billy   Soon.

Adele   I'd like to meet your dad.

Billy   You said.

Adele (*turning to him*)   Do you like him?

Billy (*stops packing, sitting*)   Sometimes. Mostly. He's been all right. My mum's a bit of a fuck-up and he's looked after me and that. Sometimes he gets angry. Sometimes he don't say nothing. For days. Just sits there staring at his toe or something. Sometimes I think he wants to fucking kill me. When he gets angry it gets quite bad. A lot of the time he just warns me about stuff and then never does anything about it. Mostly he's all right.

Adele   Did you ask him about Racheal?

Billy (*resumes packing*)   No.

Adele   My dad's a weird fucker. He says he can look into your soul.

Billy   Do you believe him?

Adele   Sometimes I do. Sometimes it's just weird. He gets really into it. He gets obsessed about things. Sometimes it seems quite believable. He told me once that I had the same powers. As he did.

Billy   Fucking hell.

Adele   I don't think it's true. But last summer I saw Racheal. Honest.

Billy   Fuck off.

Adele   I did. In our house. Running up the stairs in front of me. This was, what, two months after she died. (*Pause.*) Her mum gave me all her schoolbooks. To help me with my coursework and that. I still read them. Look at her handwriting. (*Pause.*) Billy, do you ever get the feeling that you're not allowed to be a child any more?

Billy   Why do you ask that?

Adele   It's just something my dad said to me.

Billy   No. I never feel like that.

Billy, *packed up, sits looking out over the water, away from* **Adele**.

Adele   No. Me neither. (*Beat.*) Do you know Aaron Riley?

Billy   Yeah.

Adele (*standing, straightening her skirt*)   Last Saturday yeah, he was down the Anglers. He took four pills. Four Es. In half an hour. Passed out. He had to go to hospital and have his stomach pumped. He's fifteen. I saw him at school yesterday. Asked him how he was. He said he was fine. He didn't know what all the fuss was about. Somebody asked him if he would do the same thing again. He said he didn't know. But he might do. I think he's a fucking thick cunt and he's probably going to fucking die.

Billy   Right.

Adele (*coming to join him*)   Do you know what worries me?

Billy   What?

Adele   It worries me that I've not got anything to look forward to.

Billy   That's not true.

Adele   Sometimes I think it is.

Billy   Isn't there something you've always wanted to have? Or always wanted to be.

Adele   See that's the thing. I don't think there is any more.

Billy   That's bad.

Adele   Sometimes I get so angry about stuff.

Billy   You shouldn't.

Adele   I get frustrated.

Billy   What about?

Adele   About all kinds of things. About how stupid boys our age are. I prefer twenty-year-olds, me. They know what you want. And about how petty and stupid and bitchy the girls are. I end up clenching my fists up, sometimes when I'm angry. Pull at my hair. Hit my face with my hand, hard. But that's not the same, is it? As having ambition, Billy?

Billy   Bergsie was twenty, Adele.

Adele (*walking away*)   I know.

Billy   And Ross.

Adele   I know that.

Billy (*turns to her*)   They were twenty. Did you know them?

Adele (*facing his confrontation*)   Why do you think I come here so often?

Billy   I heard that she wouldn't drown.

Adele   What?

Billy   That's what I heard. That's what the police said. That there were signs of a struggle. That she fought and kicked. So in order to keep her down under they threw rocks at her. To knock her out. And to weigh her down.

Adele   She must have realised what was happening.

Billy   She must have done.

Adele   She must have known that she was going to die.

Billy   I know.

Adele   Can you imagine?

Billy   No.

Adele   She was thirteen, Billy.

Billy   They must have been very scared.

Adele   Who?

Billy   Bergsie. Ross. The rest of them. They must have been frightened. (*Pause.*) I keep finding things. Here. Things that people have left here. Pieces of paper with phone numbers on. Photographs. Porno mags. And graffiti. And everything that I find seems to lead back to what happened to Racheal and how much she must have known –

Adele   That's bullshit.

Billy   – and what they were feeling when they realised that she was going to die. There are so many things that I find. That I come across. I don't know what to do with them all. I don't know how to make them all make sense. I end up just writing them down.

Adele   You what?

Billy   I write them down. I've got a book.

Adele (*quietly, angry*)   That's fucking weird.

Billy   No. It's not though.

Adele   Billy, it is. (*Beat.*) Do you know what I was asking about Scott for?

Billy   No.

Adele   Do you know what he did to me?

Billy   No.

Adele   He's found out about me coming here. To see you and that. So he's just been acting, like, like just a wank.

Billy   I see.

Adele   I've been off this week for three days because I've been ill. And while I've been off he's told everybody in my class that I was pregnant. Which was why I was off.

Billy   Dick.

Adele   I came into the form room this morning. And he was in there. He went into my bag when I wasn't looking and he got a tampax out of my bag and stuck it on the board. In front of everybody. He was just laughing and that. Teacher saw him and he didn't even do anything.

Billy   He's just a dick.

Adele   No. It's more than that. He keeps boasting about what happened. And joking about it being a year ago. He's a fuck. He makes people feel crippled. And people let him get away with it because they're scared of what he might do. It's just not, it's not fair, Billy. It's cruel, is what it is. And it's not enough, Billy, to just, just, just write it down, Billy. It's not enough.

Billy   What is it that you want me to do, Adele?

Adele   I don't know.

Billy   Tell me what it is that you want me to do and I'll do it. I'll honestly do anything that you ask me.

Adele   Billy.

Billy   'Cause I don't have any fucking clue for myself any more.

Adele *moves towards him but stops herself before she touches him.*

Adele   Billy, I think he's going to try to come and find you.

Long pause.

Billy   Do you know what my ambition is?

Adele   What?

Billy   I've got two.

Adele   Go on.

Billy   I want to go out to the sea. Into the ocean. With my dad. I want to see dolphins swimming, real dolphins swimming in the ocean. And I want to be able to ride on a rollercoaster. A big fucking proper one. In like Disneyland and shit. I'd fucking love that.

Aaron, Darren *and* **Scott** *have emerged from the peripheries of the stage. They are drinking bottles of Stella Artois and smoking cigarettes and scrawny joints.* **Adele** *leaves, unable to touch* **Billy**. *The lights begin to fall into evening.*

The physical gestures of the boys, especially of **Aaron**, *should be exaggerated, demonstrative.*

Aaron *(giggling, stoned, drunk)*   See that tree?

Darren *(the same, but more so)*   What?

Aaron   The fucking tree, man! See that tree?

Darren   Yeah.

Aaron   I hate that tree.

Darren   Right.

Aaron   I piss on that tree.

Darren   Right.

Aaron   Tree! I piss on you! From great, great, unthinkable heights!

Darren   Right!

Aaron   And what does the tree do?

Darren   The tree?

Aaron   What does it do?

Darren   The tree does . . .

Aaron   What does it fucking do, Darren?

Darren   Nothing.

Aaron   Fuck all.

Darren   Diddley squat.

Aaron   Stupid green motherfucker.

Darren   Star!

Aaron   See this grass?

Darren   This grass?

Aaron   I hate this grass.

Darren   Yeah, man.

Aaron   I laugh at this grass.

Darren   Excellent.

Aaron   Grass. I laugh at you! From the very bottom of my bollocks. Ha ha ha!

Darren   And I laugh at you too, grass. Ha ha ha!

Aaron   'Cause it's thick!

Darren   The grass is dumb!

Aaron   Just plain stupid.

Darren   For real.

Aaron   See these fish!

Darren   I see them.

Aaron   In the fucking canal.

Darren   I know it.

Aaron   I hate these fish!

Darren   I hate them too.

Aaron   I rape these fish!

Darren   You rape them?

Aaron   Up the batty!

Darren   Fucking thick fish!

Aaron   Waggling fish on my dick, man!

Darren   Right!

Aaron   Big fucking fish waving in the air! Flapping in the breeze.

Darren   Raped!

Aaron   Right!

Darren   Nature!

Aaron   You're thick!

Darren   Nature is thick!

Aaron   I rape it. I piss on it. And I laugh at it. (*Beat.*) Billy.

Billy (*sober*)   What?

Aaron and **Darren** *begin to close on him slightly. They pass the joint between each other.*

Aaron   You know nature, Billy?

Billy   Do I know nature?

Aaron   I hate it.

Billy   I know that.

Aaron   I rape it.

Billy   You said.

Aaron   I laugh at it. I piss on it. I think it's fucking funny.

Darren   It makes him chuckle. Giggle.

Aaron   And I think you and your dad are fucked in the head.

Darren   But we like ya.

Aaron   We do.

Darren (*offers* **Billy** *a blast on the joint,* **Billy** *ignores him*)   -
'Cause you're a funny boy.

Aaron   Nature boy!

Darren   It's lovely.

Aaron   And we like your dad.

Darren   In our own little way.

Aaron   He's all right.

Darren (*treading the joint out*)   He is.

Aaron   For a pervert.

Billy   Aaron.

Aaron   Billy.

Billy   I hope you fucking choke on your ecstasy tablets the next time you take them. I hope they stick in your throat and tear up your insides and burn up the sides of your rectum when you shit.

Billy *goes to collect his bags, tries to leave.*

Aaron   Star!

Scott (*still in the peripheries*)   Did you tell your dad, Billy?

Billy (*freezes*)   What?

Scott   Did you tell him that Ross was asking after him.

Billy (*turns to face him*)   Yeah.

Scott   And that Bergsie is set on him.

Billy   Yes. I did.

Scott   What did he say?

Billy   He's not worried.

Scott   He fucking should be.

Aaron   Damn shitting straight he should be.

Billy   He's not. He said it doesn't matter.

Darren   Did he?

Scott   I would say it mattered a lot.

Darren (*throws his beer bottle away, it smashes*)   He's a prick, man.

Scott   I would say it mattered a hell of a lot, Billy.

Billy   He said it didn't matter because they're not going to be out for ten years.

Scott   They'll be out before then, Billy.

Billy   He said they'll not be out for ten years and that we're not going to be around when they get out.

Scott   You're not going to be around?

Billy   We're going away.

Scott   Where are you going? (*No response.* **Scott** *moves in on him.*) Billy?

Billy   Southend, maybe.

Scott   What?

Billy   Or Portsmouth. Or Brighton, or Cornwall or somewhere, anywhere, somewhere by the sea. Somewhere where there's water.

Scott (*up very close*)   Is that what he said.

Billy (*not turning away*)   That's where we're going.

Scott   He said this, did he?

Billy   It's true.

Scott   When are you going there, Billy?

Billy   Soon.

Scott   Soon? Soon? Soon? When is soon, Billy. For fucksake.

Scott *moves away from* **Billy** *to enjoy the whole space.*

Aaron   He tell this to you?

Billy   Yeah.

Aaron   You believed him, Billy, did you? Did you really?

Scott   When's soon, Billy?

Billy   In a few months. After I've finished school.

Scott (*picks up* **Billy**'s *bag, feels the weight*)   He told you this, Billy. And, Billy, tell me. How is he going to afford to move you somewhere close by to the sea, Billy? How is he going to actually afford to do that exactly?

Billy   He'll get a job.

Scott   Will he? Will he really? (*Lowers his bag down.*) Fucking hell, Billy, you're a fucking wonder!

Aaron (*finishing his beer*)   I like him, Scott!

Scott   I like him too.

Aaron   I think we should keep him!

Billy   Fuck off.

A beat. **Scott** *finishes his own beer bottle, belches and throws it violently away towards the canal.*

Scott (*quietly, controlled, he moves in close to* **Billy** *again*)   Billy, let me tell you something. Can I? Billy, your dad is a fucking monkey. No one's going to give him a job, Billy. He's never going to leave this place. He's never going to leave this estate, Billy. It won't happen.

Billy   That's not true.

Scott (*gently, he maybe strokes* **Billy**'s *hair*)   It is true, Billy, of course it's fucking true, mate! And he knows it's true. You know what, Billy? He's been fucking lying to you.

Billy   No.

Scott   He's been lying because he's too scared to admit to himself, or to you, what the truth is.

Billy   No.

Scott   That he is just fucked.

Billy   No.

Scott (*prodding at, examining* **Billy**'s *face*)   And you know what, Billy, I think that you know he's been lying to you. I think that you've known all along. It's pathetic, Billy. It's fucked up, mate. It is so fucking fucked up that it's not fucking true!

Aaron *and* **Darren** *have become very still, watchful.*

Billy (*calmly, plucking up courage*)   Scott.

Scott   What?

Billy   Scott.

Scott   What?

Billy   Scott.

Scott   What?

Billy   I heard what you did.

Scott   What?

Billy   I heard what you did to Adele, Scott. And I think you're an arsehole for it, Scott. I think you're a coward. And I hope that your brother gets raped up the arse when he's in prison. Until it bleeds and fucking everything. Because he's a nonce, Scott. And everybody knows that he's a nonce. And everybody hates him and you and your whole family because of it. I hope you realise that. And I hope that you are haunted until the day you die, by the, by the, the ghost of Racheal King. And that you never forget her or what your brother did to her. And that you never, not for one second, ever know what it is to hope. I hope that happens to you, Scott. Because that is what you fucking deserve.

Scott   Billy.

Billy   Because you're a wanker.

Scott   Billy.

Billy   You're a wanker, Scott, and your brother's a nonce and everybody knows it and everybody has always known it.

Scott   Dick.

Scott *puts his fingers into* **Billy**'s *mouth, grabs hold of his cheek and pulls his head towards him. He holds the neck of his T-shirt and headbutts him twice in the face.* **Billy** *crumples and* **Scott** *pushes him to the ground. He kicks him in his side.* **Billy** *is whimpering.*

Scott (*to* **Billy**)   Shut the fuck up. (*To* **Aaron** *and* **Darren**.) Fucking hold him down.

Darren   What?

Scott   You heard me, hold him fucking down.

The two boys do and **Scott** *starts to pull* **Billy**'s *trousers down.*

Aaron (*giggling*)   What you doing, Scott?

Scott   Give me your bottle.

Aaron   You joking?

Scott   Fucking give it to me.

Billy   NO!

Scott   Give me your fucking bottle, Aaron.

He does. **Scott** *takes it and goes to force it up* **Billy**'s *rectum.* **Billy** *screams.*

Aaron   Shit, Scott, man. Take it easy, boy.

Scott   Don't you fucking tell me what to do. Don't you fucking dare tell me what to do.

Darren (*scared*)   Scott, man, please don't.

Scott (*snarled at* **Darren**)   What did you say? What did you fucking say?

Darren *and* **Aaron** *pull back, frightened by* **Scott** *and appalled by what he has done.* **Billy** *has stopped screaming and is sobbing now, hysterically but quietly. As the attack continues* **Scott** *becomes increasingly scared.*

This boy is fucking dead. He's a fucking deadbeat. This boy is a fucking deadbeat. (*To* **Billy**.) This is from Ross, Billy. A little fucking anniversary thank you. (*Rams hard once with the bottle.*) And this is from Bergsie. For everything you and your fucking dad have fucking done to my family. (*And repeats each time.*) This is from Adele. This is from your dad. And this is from your mum. And this is from your Danny. And this is from your Leanne. (*Stopping, crying.*) Nobody tells me what to do. Nobody speaks to me like that. Nobody speaks about my brother like that. Nobody speaks about my brother. Nobody speaks about me. Nobody.

Lights fade. Music briefly.

Rise on **Billy** *sitting alone, reading from his book. The lights reveal that it is a new day, perhaps some time in the afternoon. He flicks back a couple of pages, forward a couple. He starts to write something but doesn't. He closes his book. He stares out for a few moments. For a moment he seems to be watching something move on the far bank of the water.* **Adele** *joins him on stage. He doesn't acknowledge her* *approach. He sits staring out front.* **Adele** *stands behind him watching him with great caution. She speaks with great gentleness and concern. He is even, detached.*

Adele   Are you all right?

Billy   Yes.

Adele   Are you sure?

Billy   I'm fine.

Adele   I heard what they did. Aaron told me. I think you should think about phoning the police.

Billy   . . .

Adele   Billy, did it hurt you?

Billy   You know what happened when my dad phoned the police.

Adele   Did they hurt you, Billy?

Billy   Yes.

Adele   Maybe you should go to the hospital.

Billy   I'll be all right.

Adele   Maybe it will be easier when you leave.

Pause.

Billy   Maybe.

Adele *moves closer.*

Adele   He's a cunt. One day he's going to suffer. He's so going to suffer, Billy.

Billy   Yes. He will.

Adele (*edging closer*)   I used to watch him with Steph, his little sister. She's nine years old now, Billy. She's a sweet little girl. He used to punch her in the face with the ball of his hand to get her to do what he wanted her to do. And the stupid thing is that Ross was just the same with him. And he used to hate it. And his dad. You know some people can turn rooms horrible? They can twist the atmosphere of a room without actually doing anything. Scott's dad's like that. (*She sits with him, still looking at him.*) Billy I'm so sorry.

Billy   It wasn't your fault.

Pause.

Adele   Did he say anything about me?

Billy   No.

Adele   Sometimes he lies about me.

Billy   He didn't this time.

Adele   He tells people all kinds of shit.

Billy   He didn't even mention your name.

Adele   He tells people that we slept together. Which isn't true. We never did. I've never slept with anybody, Billy. I haven't. Honestly.

Billy   Why are you telling me this?

Adele   Billy, talk to me.

Billy   What do you want to talk about, Adele?

Adele   I want to make sure that you're all right. I feel guilty.

Billy   You want to feel better about it all?

Adele   Billy don't. (*Beat.*) I just want to talk to you.

Pause.

Adele   Billy, what are you going to do?

Long pause.

Billy   You should have been here earlier. There was a heron. Just sat on the other side of the canal. Down by Goresbrook House. It was magical. Sat still as stone.

Dropped into the water. Like a lead ball. Came up with a carp in between its teeth.

Adele (*turning away from him*)   I hate it when you go like this.

Billy   Like what, Adele?

Adele   I hate it when this happens.

Billy   When what happens?

Adele   I feel sick. Nervous. I feel like I'm waiting for something terrible.

Billy   Nothing terrible's going to happen, Adele.

Adele   When I was a kid, when I was little, I was suspended from my primary school. Because I took a kitchen knife into my class. And I warned people not to go near me. Because I was feeling sick and I was worried and I didn't know what I was worried about so I panicked about everybody. It felt exactly like this. It makes me feel that I'm too fat. That I'm ugly. That my skin is horrible. That my clothes are shit. It's how I feel, Billy, when I'm going to have one of my fits.

Long pause. **Billy** *looks at her for a short time. Looks away again.* **Adele** *still staring out.*

Adele (*turning to him*)   Billy. Can I see your book?

Billy (*to her*)   Why?

Adele   I want to know what it is that you write.

Billy   Why?

Adele   I want to understand how it helps.

He passes it to her. Looks back out. She opens it at the beginning. Reads a page. Flicks forward a chunk. And back. Reading random pages with great care.

Adele   What are these numbers at the end of each day?

Billy   They're all the people who have passed by where I fish. I count them.

Adele   Why?

Billy   I have no idea.

She reads more.

Adele   You write down all the graffiti.

Billy   . . .

She reads more.

Adele   I like this. Can I read a bit to you. 'Some of the people look like sticks. They look like they could snap. They have nodules in odd places.' I think that's very true.

She finds a new passage and reads it with care.

Adele   'When the sky gets blue like this it makes the colours on the buildings seem more acute. The orange of the chemist. The blue colour of the bookies.' (*Beat.*) Who's Leanne? And Danny?

Billy   They're my brother and sister.

Adele   I didn't know you had a brother and a sister.

Billy   They live with my mum.

Adele   Do they? How come?

Billy   They're younger than I am.

Adele   So?

Billy   I decided that I wanted to leave and come and live with my dad. They were too young to decide for themselves. So they stayed. I don't see them very often.

Adele   Do you miss them?

Billy   Yeah. I do.

Adele   Why don't you go and see them?

Billy   Because then I'd have to see my mum and I really don't want to see her.

Adele   Why not?

Billy (*as though confused by the question, it's so obvious*)   Because I hate her, Adele.

Adele   Why?

Billy (*almost spat at her*)   Why do *you* want to know?

Adele (*not flinching*)   Don't be angry.

They establish and then maintain eye contact.

Billy   I've got every right to be angry. Why do you want to know about my mum?

Adele   I just want to talk to you.

Billy   I hate her because she's vicious. She's horrible. She's horrible to me. And she's horrible to Danny and Leanne and she was horrible to my dad.

Adele   Was she?

Billy   She's a wino. A pisshead. A cruel drunken bitch.

Adele *lets him continue.*

Billy   One time, when she'd been on the drink, she hit me. She beat me up. She did. She got my head by my hair, this is, what, when I was nine years old. She got my head by my hair and she smacked it against the radiator in our front room until I was sick and until my head started to bleed. So I rang my dad up and told him what happened and he came to get me. And now he looks after me. Danny and Leanne were too young to come with us.

Adele   Fucking hell, Billy.

Billy   What?

Adele   I never realised.

Billy   People say all this stuff about Dad and what he's like and what he does. And none of it is ever true, Adele. They don't have the slightest idea.

Adele   Have you told him what happened?

Billy   No.

Adele   Maybe you should tell him.

Billy (*turns away*)   No.

Adele   Billy.

Billy   Do you know what I want most of all in the world?

Adele   What?

Billy   I want him to be all right. I want him to get over everything that Mum did to him. And I want him to get over, to just get over finding Racheal.

Adele   It won't happen.

Billy   What?

Adele   He won't get over finding Racheal. People don't get over something like that.

He refuses to look back to her so she returns to the book. She finds something there.

Adele   What's this?

Billy   Do you know what worries me?

Adele   What's this, Billy?

Billy   It worries me that I'm going to end up like him. Broken up like that.

Adele   Billy, what's this about?

Billy   What?

Adele (*reading*)   'She stands for maybe thirty seconds and then carries on walking. Doesn't say anything. Sometimes she looks at me or at Dad. She has blonde hair. Huge eyes.

She looks very sad and she looks fragile sometimes, like an egg shell. And other times she looks hard and cruel.' Billy? 'She has a small scar underneath her right eye. I watch the way she moves. I watch the rise and fall of her breathing. And the way her legs move when she walks. I watch her all the time.'

Billy (*standing, going for the book*)   Don't read that bit.

Adele (*standing with him, guarding it*)   Billy, is this about me?

Billy   Can I have my book back please, Adele?

Adele   Have you been writing about me, Billy?

Billy   Give me my book back.

Adele   Billy.

Face to face. Close.

Billy   What?

Adele   What is it that you want from me?

Billy   I just want. I just don't want you to go.

Michelle *enters. She pulls out a cigarette. Some time.* **Adele** *keeps watching* **Billy** *closely.*

Michelle   Is that a new jacket, Billy? It suits you. You look really smart, darling.

Billy   Mum.

Adele *leaves. She straightens the collar of* **Billy**'s *jacket before she does.* **Billy** *turns to his mum.*

Michelle   You always did used to look after your clothes, didn't you? You always took such a lot of pride in your, in your appearance. What you wore. Your hair, all of that. I remember.

Billy (*moving to her*)   Mum I want to see Danny and Leanne.

Michelle (*joining him, moves to touch him but he gives nothing*)
They want to see you too, Billy. They ask about you all the
time.

Billy (*standing firm*) Because we're going away. Me and
Dad. We're going away and I want to see them to tell them
where we're going and how they can get in touch with me.

Michelle I see.

Billy (*still*) But I don't want to come round.

Michelle Where are you going?

Billy I'm not going to come round to the house so I need
you to give a message to them.

Michelle (*lights the cigarette*) Where are you going, Billy,
the two of you?

Billy I'm not going to tell you, Mum.

Michelle What?

Billy I don't have to. I shouldn't even be here. If Dad
knew I was talking to you he'd go, he'd . . . He'd kill you.

Michelle Why won't you tell me where you're going,
Billy?

Billy Because where we go, you're never going to find us.
I'm not going to let you.

Michelle (*replacing her lighter*) Billy, doll, don't be silly.

Billy I'm not being silly, Mum, I'm being serious. (*Beat.
Closer still.*) Will you tell them to come and meet me?

Michelle You can't stop me coming to see you, Billy . . .

Billy I can, Mum. And I will. Will you tell them?

Michelle (*doing up her coat*) How can you?

Billy Will you?

Michelle (*perplexed, not bitter, moving slightly away from him*)
How can you do this?

Billy   What?

Michelle (*turns back*)   How can you have become so hard?

Billy   You what?

Michelle   You never even talk to me.

Billy   Mum.

Michelle   You look at me as though you hate me.

Billy   After everything you did.

Michelle   Billy, what – ?

Billy (*cutting her off*)   You hit me so hard that it made me
sick.

Beat. They talk over each other.

Billy   You used to say such terrible, horrible fucked-up
just fucking shit –

Michelle   And I'm sorry, Billy, please –

Billy   – And what you did to Dad.

Michelle   To Charlie?

Billy   When you were on the drink, Mum, you did so
many things that were just disgusting. Despicable.

Michelle (*over his next speech*)   Billy. Billy. Billy. Billy.

Face to face.

Billy (*bursting with a need to tell her*)   I remember, do you
remember, that time, after Dad moved out, when you
brought those fellas round. Those two bastards from
Kempton's Bar? And told Dad to come and see you. And
they were waiting there. When he arrived. They were
waiting for him. Do you remember that?

Michelle   Billy.

Billy They had bicycle chains, Mum, didn't they and they just fucking beat him up so badly and I was watching. I was watching all the time. You knew I was and you still let them do it.

Michelle (*moving closer*) I didn't know.

Billy Of course you knew!

Michelle Billy.

Billy (*containing himself*) Will you give Danny and Leanne a message?

Michelle (*treads her cigarette out*) You're not going anywhere.

Billy I want them to come and meet me. Here. At three-thirty tomorrow.

Michelle (*smiling, moving towards him*) Charlie won't take you anywhere.

Billy (*standing defiant*) He will.

Michelle Charlie won't leave.

Billy He will.

Michelle He couldn't.

Billy He's going to.

Michelle He couldn't. He couldn't, Billy, because he couldn't leave me.

Billy (*exasperated, perhaps looking around as though trying to find somewhere to run to*) What? What are you talking about?

Michelle (*close up*) He couldn't leave me, Billy. He needs me too much.

Billy You're cracking up, Mum.

Michelle (*calm, gentle*) I'm not, Billy. He needs me too much. He loves me too much. Billy, he rings me all the time, love.

Billy   No he doesn't.

Michelle (*standing the collar of his jacket up*)   Billy, love, I'm not going to lie to you.

Billy   He doesn't.

Michelle (*very gently, perhaps stroking his face*)   He does. He speaks to Danny and Leanne. He talks to me for hours. He told me that he wanted to see me again. He won't leave, Billy, he just won't.

Billy (*backing off but not turning away*)   Fuck off.

Michelle   Billy.

Billy   Just fuck off. You liar. You fucking lying cunt.

Michelle   Billy.

His movements become slightly hysterical. Perhaps he hits himself as he backs off.

Billy   He wouldn't do that to me, after everything you did to me? No way would he do that. No way would he do that. You fucking lying bitch cunt.

Michelle   Billy, don't go.

Billy *moves away.* **Michelle** *watches him as he grabs his diary, opens it, and grasping his pen in the fist of his hand writes down his furious last note. She leaves gently. He reads some of his writing out loud as he writes. Perhaps he becomes isolated by light. He is exhausted. Gathers his breath. He speaks hurriedly. Pausing to recover his breath at points. His voice occasionally breaking. Perhaps bent over as though suffering from a stitch.*

Billy   This is the final entry into this journal. It is Friday. Today the sky is more purely blue than I can remember seeing it before. It seems terrible and huge and magnificent. This is everything.

He begins to change from writing into scribbling. Vicious sharp lines that almost tear the pages. And shaking he starts to tear up the pages of his book.

Isolating light falls on **Billy**.

Darkness. Perhaps music.

The lights rise again with **Aaron**, **Darren** *and* **Scott** *sat around the stage. Still drinking. Still smoking.* **Darren** *rolls a scrawny joint.* **Billy**, *some distance behind them, holds his dad's gun to* **Scott**'s *head. Until he speaks the boys don't notice him. He speaks calmly. He chooses his words with great care and he reasons with very simple, straightforward logic.* **Scott** *doesn't pay any attention at first. Perhaps we don't see the gun for a few moments.*

Billy   You need to apologise to me.

Aaron (*seeing the gun, confused*)   Billy?

Billy   You need to apologise to me.

Darron (*seeing the gun, alarmed*)   Fucking hell.

Scott   What?

Billy   What you did to me was unforgivable.

Scott *turns around and sees the gun.* **Aaron** *and* **Darren** *are slightly paralysed by surprise.*

Scott   Billy, for fucksake.

Billy (*interrupting him, calmly reasoning, pointing the gun clearly now*)   What you did, the things which you did. You shouldn't treat people like that.

Scott   Christ, Billy, is that real?

Billy (*coming forward*)   It's my dad's. He uses it for shooting herons because they kill his fish. And he uses it for protection against robbers. And if you don't apologise to me, Scott, I'm going to shoot you in your head.

Scott (*scrambling backwards*)   For fucksake, Billy, what . . .

Billy   For all this time. For all the money I've given you. For all the things that have happened here. All the things which you have said to me. All the things which you have done and which Aaron and Darren have done to try to impress you.

Scott   Billy, please.

Billy   And the things which you've said about my dad. And the things which you've said about my mum. And my brother and my sister.

Scott (*becoming more frightened*)   Oh! Fucking fuck.

Billy   And the things which you did to Adele.

Scott   No. No. No. No.

Billy   And what you did to me. Scott. What you did to me. You need to apologise to me for these things. Because it's just not fair. It's just not right, Scott.

Scott   I wasn't . . .

Billy   You need to apologise, Scott.

Scott   I'm sorry. I'm sorry. I'm sorry. I'm sorry. It wasn't me.

Billy   How do you know about my brother and sister, Scott?

Scott   What?

Billy   You heard me.

Scott   My sister knows them. My sister knows your Leanne. They're in the same class together. At primary school.

Billy *takes this in for a while. Might be backing off and then . . .*

Billy (*closing in*)   What did you mean it wasn't you, Scott?

Scott (*terrified now*)   I mean, I, I don't know. I mean. Shit. Please don't kill me.

Billy (*tighter*)   What did you mean it wasn't you?

Scott (*folding in on himself*)   I try. I try. I try. I try. I lose my temper. I try really hard to, to just. I try so fucking hard Billy but it's so fucked.

Billy   What is?

Scott   It's so mad. Please. It's just difficult because it's so. Terrible.

Billy   What is, Scott?

Scott   With, with, with Ross and with what you said and what happened and all that shit. People don't. Please don't, don't, don't hurt me, Billy.

Billy   That's not enough.

Scott   Please don't hurt me, Billy.

Billy   It's not enough.

Aaron (*frightened, maybe crying*)   Billy.

Darren (*the same*)   Billy, don't, for fucksake.

They perhaps move towards him, very cautious.

Billy   Shut up, fucking shut up just, honestly, just shut up. Or I swear I'll, I'll, I will kill him.

They freeze.

Scott   Please. I'm so sorry.

Billy   Are you scared, Scott?

Scott   What?

Billy   Are you scared?

Scott   Yes.

Billy   How scared are you, Scott?

Scott   I'm not my brother. I'm not my dad. I'm not . . .

Billy   Answer my question.

Scott   I'm so very scared. I don't want to die, Billy.

Billy   I've nothing left to lose, Scott.

Scott   Please, Billy.

Billy (*standing almost over him, like an executioner*)   I've nothing left to lose any more. You took it all away from me, Scott. You and your brother. And what you did to my dad. And my mum. And this place. And all of this.

Scott   I'm only fifteen, Billy.

Billy   I'm fucking fourteen, Scott, you idiot.

Billy *pulls the trigger. The first chamber on the barrel is empty.* **Scott** *is terrified. A sharp, loud intake of breath.*

Scott *sobs hysterically, pleading.* **Aaron** *and* **Darren** *are petrified.*

Scott   Please. Billy, Billy, Billy, please. I don't want to die, Billy. I want to live, Billy.

Billy   What for, Scott?

He pulls the trigger for the second time. Again an empty chamber. Another gasp for breath from **Scott**.

Billy   There's nothing left for us now, Scott, is there?

He pulls the trigger for the third time. The chamber is again empty.

A moment. **Scott** *sobbing.* **Aaron** *and* **Darren** *stunned.* **Billy** *in total control. He grins.*

The sound of the water in the lock.

The lights fade to darkness.

They rise fairly quickly.

Billy *sits alone on stage. It is the morning. He stares out to the audience for some moments. Exhausted. Frightened. Moved.*

Adele *joins him. She is extremely cautious. Moves towards him.*

Adele   Billy?

Billy   Yeah?

Adele   Did you kill him?

Long pause.

Billy   I saw my mum last night.

Adele (*moving closer*)   Oh yeah?

Billy   I told her to tell Leanne and Danny to come here. At three-thirty. I hope she told them.

Adele   Did you kill him, Billy?

Billy   She was funny. She made me laugh. With her fucking stupid coat on and that.

Adele   Billy.

Billy   I don't want to talk about it, Adele.

Pause.

Billy (*looking away*)   If you could be any animal in the world, Adele. Any animal at all, other than a human being, what would you be?

Adele (*looking away*)   I don't know. A cat.

Billy (*looking to* **Adele**)   Why?

Adele   Just so you can sleep and that.

Billy (*looking away*)   I'd be a fish, I reckon.

Adele   Why would you be a fish?

Billy   Because they have no memory. They just swim around. If you have no memory you're never frightened about stuff.

Adele (*looking to* **Billy**)   What are you frightened about, Billy?

Billy   Everything that I can remember.

Adele   Everything?

Billy   Cats eat fish.

Adele   Everything, Billy?

Billy   But then cats are scared of water so I'd be able to swim away. (*Looking to* **Adele**.) Are you all right?

Adele   Am I all right?

Billy   Last time I saw you you said you were feeling nervous. Anxious.

Adele   No . . .

Billy   You said you felt like you felt when you were going to have a fit.

Pause.

Adele   I think I'm fine now, Billy, thanks. I think it's passed.

Billy (*new thought*)   Aren't you?

Adele   What?

Billy   Frightened of the things you can remember?

Adele   Some things. But some things I'm not.

Billy   Which ones aren't you?

Adele   I remember when my niece was born. I was there. I saw her getting born. That wasn't frightening. That was amazing.

Billy   Was it?

Adele   It was beautiful.

Billy   How old is she now?

Adele   She's three years old. I love her, y'know? She's very enthusiastic about things. (*Beat.*) Have the police been round?

Billy   It's a good age, Adele, isn't it?

Adele   Have they?

Billy (*looking away*)   It is, though, isn't it? That age? Don't you think? It's very creative.

Adele   Billy?

Billy   Can I ask you a question?

Adele   You answer mine first.

Billy (*looking back to* **Adele**)   Mine's important.

Adele   Have the police been round, Billy?

Billy   I don't know. I've not been home. I've not seen my dad. If they'd been he'd come and find me.

Adele   Did you kill him, Billy?

Billy   You said I could ask my question.

Adele   Did you shoot him?

Billy   You promised.

Adele   Go on.

Billy   Where did you get your scar from? On your cheek?

Adele (*after a beat*)   When my dad found out that I knew Bergsie and Ross, after I told him about Racheal's ghost, he smacked me with his belt.

Billy   Across your face?

Adele (*looking away*)   He just gets angry with stuff.

Billy   I see.

Adele   It doesn't worry me.

Billy   What was he like?

Adele   Who?

Billy   Bergsie?

Adele   You have to answer my second question first. Before I answer yours.

Billy   No. You first this time, Adele. What was he like?

Adele   He was very quiet. He didn't say much. I think he was nervous a lot of the time. I never found out about where he came from or anything but I always had the impression that it was horrible.

Billy   How?

Adele   Just the way he moved and stuff. He always looked frightened that anything could happen.

Billy (*also looking away*)   I used to think Scott was like that.

Adele   No. Not Scott. (*Looking at* **Billy**.) Scott was nowhere near. You answer my question now. (*Pause.*) Billy. (*Pause.*) Did you kill Scott?

Some time. **Billy** *looks away out to the audience.* **Adele** *watches him.*

Billy   No. Of course I didn't.

Adele   Thank God, Billy.

Billy   Why?

Adele   Just thank God, is all.

Billy   It was funny.

Adele   What?

Billy   He wanted so badly to live, Adele.

Adele   What?

Billy   He was crying. Like a little baby and everything.

Adele   Billy . . .

Billy   I thought there must be a reason for him wanting to stay alive so badly.

Adele   He was scared you were going to shoot him in the head.

Billy   I was thinking about Ross, Adele, and Bergsie. I think I know why they were so scared. I think that they realised what I realised when I saw Scott like that. The way that things are wonderful. The way that colours work. The sound of things and the way they smell, Adele. But they couldn't handle it. So they got frightened. And I started to figure out how everything joins up, Adele.

Adele   What?

Billy   The blue sky. And the flowers in the towpath.

Adele   What?

Billy   Everything is just joined up. . .

Pause. He looks to her.

Billy   Adele, I'm so glad you stayed.

Adele   I wanted to check that you were all right. I wanted to find out if you'd hurt him or if you'd got hurt. Or if the police had found you.

Billy   I was thinking about my test. I was trying to figure out what I'd say if I got asked if I deserved to go to heaven or if I should really go to hell. I think I deserve to go to heaven I do. I think I really fucking do and all.

She holds his eye contact. He looks away again.

Billy   If the police find me, if they come, what do you think they'll do?

Adele   I don't know.

Billy (*back to her*)   Do you think that this means that I won't be able to leave here now, Adele?

Charlie *arrives on stage and moves slowly to join* **Billy** *and* **Adele**. **Adele** *sees him first. For a long time very little is said. It should be clear that* **Charlie** *knows that something bad has happened. There is a difference, a caution in the way that he moves or the way that he looks at his son that we haven't seen before. We can infer from this that the police have been round. He sits down next to*

Billy. *The three of them look out at the canal together.* **Charlie** *rolls a cigarette but doesn't light it.*

Charlie   Billy.

Billy   Dad.

Charlie (*to* **Billy**)   You all right?

Billy (*to his dad*)   I'm fine, yeah.

Charlie   Good man.

Charlie *goes to light his cigarette but is interrupted by* **Billy**.

Billy   This is Adele.

Charlie   Sorry?

Billy   This is my friend Adele, Dad.

Charlie   Oh. All right, Adele.

Adele   All right.

Long pause. They look out again. This time his memory stops
Charlie *from lighting up.*

Charlie   Funny.

Billy   What is?

Charlie   I was thinking. On the way here.

Billy   What?

Charlie   Used to come here when you was a baby.
Sometimes. If I, like, if I was looking after you for the day
and that. I'd bring you down here. Used to look at the birds
and that. See if we could see the ducks. And the herons and
everything. You used to love all that. When you was just like
a little baby and everything. (*Pause.*) Billy.

Billy   Yeah.

Charlie   Billy, the, er, the police come round.

Billy   I see.

Charlie (*looking to* **Billy**)   They told us what happened, Billy.

Billy   Right.

Charlie   Billy, what have you done, mate?

Billy (*turns to his dad*)   Dad I didn't touch him. Dad I didn't do nothing. I just . . .

Charlie   Billy.

Billy   I fucked it up, Dad. I'm sorry.

Charlie   Yeah, I know you are, son. It's all right.

Billy   Is it?

Charlie   Where's the gun, Billy, where d'you put the gun?

Billy (*looks out*)   I threw it in the canal.

Charlie (*slight laugh*)   Did you?

Billy   Yeah.

Charlie (*looks out*)   Right.

Long pause.

Billy (*looks to his dad*)   I saw Mum again, Dad. Yesterday. Dad, do you still ring her?

Charlie (*faces him*)   What?

Billy   Do you ring her, on the telephone? Speak to her and Leanne and Danny?

Charlie   No.

Billy   It's just what she said.

Charlie   It's not true.

Billy   Good, I'm glad. (*Beat. They both look out again.*) What did you tell the police?

Charlie   I told them to fuck off. That I hadn't seen you for two years. That you lived with your mum and I asked them if they could leave me alone and stop causing me so much anxiety.

Billy   Right.

Charlie (*looking to him*)   Do you know what I like about you?

Billy   What?

Charlie   You're very straightforward. You're very honest. It makes you seem quite, like, quite simple.

Billy   Right. (*Pause. Half turns to him.*) Dad.

Charlie   Yeah.

Billy   Dad, I've decided. I'm going. When the summer comes. When school's finished. I'm leaving. I just, I just am.

Charlie   I see.

Billy   I can't stay here for ever, Dad. It's just too difficult.

Charlie   I know.

Billy   You can come with me if you want to but I'm definitely, I'm just definitely just going.

Charlie   Right.

Billy   I'm going to go to Southend, I think. Or Brighton. Or Portsmouth. Somewhere where there's sea.

Charlie   I think that's a good idea, Billy.

Long pause. All three looking out.

Billy   Should we go home now?

Charlie   Yeah, let's go home.

There is a long pause as the three of them stare out front. Occasionally **Adele** *glances at the two of them. Occasionally* **Billy** *catches her glance. Lights fade. 'Can I Pass?' by The Rebel plays to close.*

Methuen Contemporary Dramatists
include

Peter Barnes (three volumes)
Sebastian Barry
Edward Bond (six volumes)
Howard Brenton
  (two volumes)
Richard Cameron
Jim Cartwright
Caryl Churchill (two volumes)
Sarah Daniels (two volumes)
Nick Darke
David Edgar (three volumes)
Ben Elton
Dario Fo (two volumes)
Michael Frayn (two volumes)
Paul Godfrey
John Guare
Peter Handke
Jonathan Harvey
Declan Hughes
Terry Johnson (two volumes)
Bernard-Marie Koltès
David Lan
Bryony Lavery
Doug Lucie
David Mamet (three volumes)

Martin McDonagh
Duncan McLean
Anthony Minghella
  (two volumes)
Tom Murphy (four volumes)
Phyllis Nagy
Anthony Nielsen
Philip Osment
Louise Page
Joe Penhall
Stephen Poliakoff
  (three volumes)
Christina Reid
Philip Ridley
Willy Russell
Ntozake Shange
Sam Shepard (two volumes)
Wole Soyinka (two volumes)
David Storey (three volumes)
Sue Townsend
Michel Vinaver (two volumes)
Michael Wilcox
David Wood (two volumes)
Victoria Wood

METHUEN STUDENT EDITIONS

☐ SERJEANT MUSGRAVE'S DANCE	John Arden	£6.99
☐ CONFUSIONS	Alan Ayckbourn	£5.99
☐ THE ROVER	Aphra Behn	£5.99
☐ LEAR	Edward Bond	£6.99
☐ THE CAUCASIAN CHALK CIRCLE	Bertolt Brecht	£6.99
☐ MOTHER COURAGE AND HER CHILDREN	Bertolt Brecht	£6.99
☐ THE CHERRY ORCHARD	Anton Chekov	£5.99
☐ TOP GIRLS	Caryl Churchill	£6.99
☐ A TASTE OF HONEY	Shelagh Delaney	£6.99
☐ STRIFE	John Galsworthy	£5.99
☐ ACROSS OKA	Robert Holman	£5.99
☐ A DOLL'S HOUSE	Henrik Ibsen	£5.99
☐ MY MOTHER SAID I NEVER SHOULD	Charlotte Keatley	£6.99
☐ DREAMS OF ANNE FRANK	Bernard Kops	£5.99
☐ BLOOD WEDDING	Federico García Lorca	£5.99
☐ THE HOUSE OF BERNARD ALBA	Federico García Lorca	£7.99
☐ THE MALCONTENT	John Marston	£5.99
☐ BLOOD BROTHERS	Willy Russell	£6.99
☐ DEATH AND THE KING'S HORSEMAN	Wole Soyinka	£6.99
☐ THE PLAYBOY OF THE WESTERN WORLD	J. M. Synge	£5.99
☐ OUR COUNTRY'S GOOD	Timberlake Wertenbaker	£6.99
☐ THE IMPORTANCE OF BEING ERNEST	Oscar Wilde	£7.99
☐ BLUE MURDER	Peter Nichols	£5.99
☐ A STREETCAR NAMED DESIRE	Tennessee Williams	£5.99

* All Methuen Drama books are available through mail order or from your local bookshop, or online at www.methuen.co.uk.

Please send cheque/eurocheque/postal order (sterling only) Access, Visa, Mastercard, Diners Card, Switch or Amex.

Expiry Date: .... Signature: ....

Please allow 75 pence per book for post and packing U.K.
Overseas customers please allow £1.00 per copy for post and packing.
ALL ORDERS TO:
Methuen Books, Books by Post, TBS Limited, The Book Service, Colchester Road, Frating Green, Colchester, Essex CO7 7DW.

NAME: ....

ADDRESS: ....

....

....

Please allow 28 days for delivery. Please tick box if you do not ☐
wish to receive any additional information

Prices and availability subject to change without notice.

Methuen Film *titles include*

The Wings of the Dove
Hossein Armini

Mrs Brown
Jeremy Brock

Persuasion
Nick Dear after Jane Austen

The Gambler
Nick Dear after Dostoyevsky

Beautiful Thing
Jonathan Harvey

Little Voice
Mark Herman

The Long Good Friday
Barrie Keeffe

The Crucible
Arthur Miller

The English Patient
Anthony Minghella

Twelfth Night
Trevor Nunn after Shakespeare

The Krays
Philip Ridley

The Reflecting Skin & The Passion of Darkly Noon
Philip Ridley

Trojan Eddie
Billy Roche

Sling Blade
Billy Bob Thornton

The Acid House
Irvine Welsh

For a complete catalogue of Methuen Drama titles
write to:

Methuen Drama
215 Vauxhall Bridge Road
London SW1V 1EJ

or you can visit our website at:

www.methuen.co.uk

Printed in the United Kingdom
by Lightning Source UK Ltd.
122052UK00001B/178/A